Sacred
Living

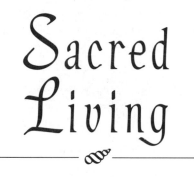

Sacred Living

A DAILY GUIDE

ROBIN HEERENS LYSNE

CONARI PRESS
Berkeley, California

Grateful acknowledgment is given for an excerpt from
Talking with Our Brothers by George M. Taylor.
Reprinted by permission of the Men's Community Publishing Project.

Conari Press books are distributed by Publishers Group West.

Cover design: Ame Beanland
Cover illustration: Roger Montoya
Interior design and composition: Suzanne Albertson

ISBN: 1-57324-099-0

Library of Congress Cataloging-in-Publication Data
Lysne, Robin Heerens, 1953-
Sacred living : a daily guide / by Robin Heerens Lysne.
p.   cm.
Includes bibliographical references and index.
ISBN 1-57324-099-0
1. Spiritual life.   2. Devotional calendars.   I. Title.
BL624.L97   1997
291.4'4—dc21   97-15645
                    CIP

Printed in the United States of America on recycled paper
10 9 8 7 6 5 4 3 2 1

This book is in honor of my parents,
Robert and Martha,
who taught me how to live
a sacred life.

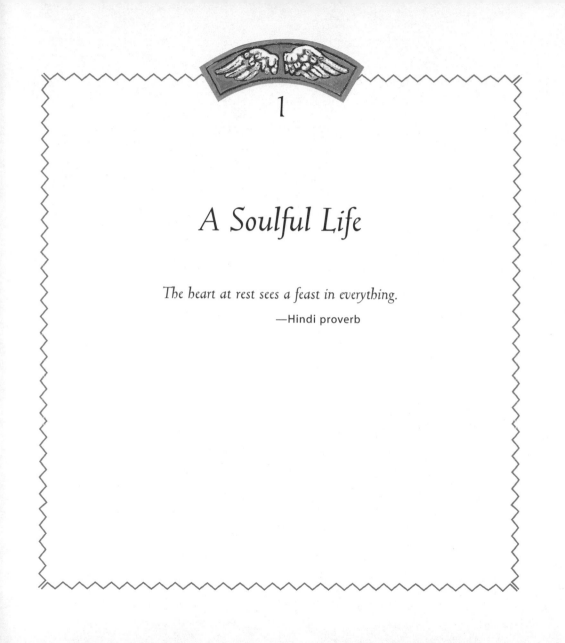

1

A Soulful Life

The heart at rest sees a feast in everything.

—Hindi proverb

WHAT IS SACRED LIVING? It is aligning our living with the rhythms of the Earth and recognizing that those rhythms are sacred. For the closer we get to the Earth, the closer we get to the great mystery.

Sacred living is living in the knowledge that we are part of something larger than ourselves. It is being grateful for life while we live it. It is observing and celebrating changes as they come every day, whether they are seasonal or personal. It is being with what is and creating commemorative moments through rituals or ceremonies when it feels right.

Many religions have maligned our physical existence as something apart from God. This is contrary to the view of a self-organizing, self-rectifying Universe that scientists are beginning to acknowledge as they observe nature with greater and greater technological awareness and awe.

We do not, however, need science to validate what we know is true in our very bones. Life is a mystery—awe inspiring like nothing humans can create or invent. It is self-cleansing, self-balancing, and constantly nurturing. Celebrating that mystery brings us into closer communion with life and with each other. Our ancestors have known this for centuries. All celebrations throughout the history of the world are tied to the cycles of the Earth and the seasons of food production. We have forgotten this only in recent times.

Seasons of Change

Through our high-tech culture and delusional thinking that somehow man has dominion over nature, we have become out of touch with the natural law and order in the Universe. The word dominion originally came from the root word dominus—which meant stewardship, not domination as it has come to be translated and used. The Old French *demaine* meant learned borrowing, while the latin *domus* meant house and *dominus* meant master or lord. Nature is our house, the master from which we borrow in a learned fashion, so as not to disturb the balance.

Unfortunately, we have tampered and manipulated nature to such an extent that we have dismantled the very systems that worked flawlessly without our interference for millions of years before the arrival of humans. Now we are in jeopardy of committing suicide with our environment and our lives. This is why I have emphasized ways in *Sacred Living* to realign ourselves with nature.

The seasons inform us of natural law. They are a perfect metaphor for, as well as actual demonstration of, natural order. "To all things there is a season..." were the lyrics of a famous Byrds song taken from the book of Ecclesiastes 3:1–8, and paying attention to the changing seasons helps us stay in tune to our own inner changes. While we watch the changes outside ourselves, we can also feel the movement of change inside ourselves.

Each season has its own quality. Winter, a time of going inside, is the season of faith; spring is the season of promise; summer is the season of growth; and autumn is the season of abundance. Every season also exhibits references to the three forces in the Universe—dynamic, magnetic, and integrative. As the sun reaches its extremes in summer and winter, both masculine and feminine aspects are present. These are times of extremes and times of equal power. The autumn (autumnal) and spring (vernal) equinox are more integrative times. Because they are seasons of turbulent weather, they tend to be more unstable transitional times.

〰 Balancing Masculine and Feminine 〰

I use the terms masculine *and* feminine *to describe two types of energy found universally. The masculine principle is active or dynamic energy. The feminine is magnetic or reflective energy. Both are very important in understanding spirit and ourselves. I use these terms in the energetic sense rather than as a reference to male and female genders, for both men and women have both aspects in their nature. Male and female sexuality, however, play an important part in the expression of these two dynamic factors.*

In Chinese wisdom teaching, the yin (feminine energy) and the yang (masculine energy) are what balance a person, symbolized by the yin/yang symbol. In western culture, we too often regard only the masculine principle, without regard to the feminine. In order to come into balance, whether we are men or women, we must integrate both masculine and feminine into our lives.

The more in touch we are with nature, the more we can appreciate with wonder the incredible timing of the Earth. Through its cycles, we can acknowledge more of creation in all its beauty, fierceness, and gentle unfolding.

Seasons of Change Within

As we become more in tune with the seasons, we also become more in touch with our natural rhythms, both physical or emotional. Eating, sleeping, exercising, playing, and loving are all gifts—the simplest things can be part of our spiritual lives if we intend them to be. Crying is a gift of cleansing. Pain is a gift signaling lessons. Anger is a gift and a warning signal of boundaries crossed.

In each season, the one thing to keep in mind is that change is the only constant. There is no stopping the cycle of birth, growth, flowering, death, and rebirth. Within our own lives, the process of regeneration takes place in the same way as the seasons. If we do not listen to our own seasons, we fall out of balance, out of harmony with life. This, I believe is the major cause of disorder and disease in our culture. To realign ourselves, we must first slow down and give ourselves enough time and space to be with what is both inside and outside.

When we are in touch with our bodies, we become in touch with the natural rhythms of life imbedded in our bones and tissues. The more aware of this we are, the more we begin to understand that we are integrally connected to the air and water, Earth and sun. We begin to understand that our survival depends on nature, that we are supported by it.

And if we listen to our bodies and the body of the Earth, we will know what is going on around us and in us.

It is humbling to be one with nature. Indeed, the root of the word humility is *humus*—Earth; to become humble is to get close to the Earth. Humility requires us to surrender and change, to focus on the nonmaterial gifts that life offers us every day.

A soulful life requires being aware that we are a soul in a body, which is connected to the bigger body of the Earth and the Universe. At the same time, it is noticing the miracles of your functioning body, of your children or other loved ones, of how you are feeling and watching the changes in yourself from moment to moment.

Whether you have a religious tradition or not, everyone has to define meaning in his or her unique way. For some, meditation is essential to spiritual practicing. For others, playing with their kids, working, exercising, singing, breathing, fighting, praying, attending religious services, dancing, lovemaking, or any combination of these activities may bring them into relationship with the Universe. The truth is, anything you do in your daily life can be a part of practicing presence.

Because change is the catalyst for soul growth, transitional times are the most difficult to stay present in. They are the times when we live most unconsciously, because we fall back on what's familiar. Sometimes we fall asleep to the decisions we make, the outdated myths we are reinforcing in ourselves, or the dramas we are playing out over and over again. During transitions, we are forced to let go of old systems of belief, attachments to possessions, locations, or relationships that no longer serve us. Acquiring a new relationship, place to live, or work can be challenging to beliefs or habits that were formed around past experiences.

Creating rites or celebrations during times of change helps us stay conscious of what we are doing during a transition. Paying attention reveals the divine drama of our soul's growth, as we come to understand that everything in our lives has a purpose, with a meaningful lesson folded into it. Falling apart or losing a job can be just what the soul needs. With such openness to the spirit's living through us, there is room for every experience, every occurrence, every feeling. We make peace with being here, learning the lessons we have to face. We move away from denial and into what *is*. Indeed, we begin to see that we are the Universe looking, appreciating, loving, and living itself.

Spiritual practice helps us listen to life for answers. We learn that we can ask for help, knowing that we will receive the help we need. We move into dynamic harmony with all things. We also learn that our attitudes and beliefs shape what we receive and whether we feel deserving of the abundant good available to us or not.

If you are reading this book you probably have already experienced something of the sacred, and you want more of it. I believe everyone has his or her own inner wisdom and unique path to follow. You know what is right and most significant for you. My intention is to inspire and empower you to find your own way, not to create a new dogma or sell a new theology.

In this book, you will find ways to live more soulfully that extend naturally from what you already do. By sharing my experiences, I hope to point you in a direction that may bring more meaning to your life.

It is my greatest joy to share with you ways to honor the sacred.

The process has helped me love myself and others more and bring loved ones closer together. It has shifted the emphasis in my life from a material-based existence, where my self-esteem and measure of success were based largely on my income, to a spiritual one, where I know I am sacred and the world around me is too, and I live out of that knowing.

The body of the book is meant to inspire you in your daily life. Each day, it offers a word for your contemplation and an affirmation for you to work with. The purpose of these is to focus you on a particular aspect of the sacred. Also included are suggestions for creating special moments of peace and reflection in your busy day.

Throughout *Sacred Living* there are also seasonal suggestions to help you mark important turning points in your life. To do this is to create a rite of passage, a phrase coined by anthropologist Arnold Van Gennep in his 1906 book, *Rites of Passage*. The word rite or ritual comes from the Latin word *ritus* or river. Life force or spirit is like a river that flows through every living thing. When we take time to mark a passage or create a ritual, we are dipping into the river of life. In his book *Reinventing Work*, Matthew Fox states: "Only ritual teaches us to honor the sacred." When we are the creators of ceremonies that celebrate the changes that happen every day, we make connections, bond our families, and mark life passages. We bless our bodies, minds, and souls. We celebrate; we grieve; we share our journey with those we love.

While this is a daily guide, the emphasis is on how to use the daily inspirational messages and practices of meditation and prayer to check in with yourself and your relationship and make you more aware of what is all around you throughout the year. The seasons here are both literal and metaphoric. That's why there is an index at the back of the book. It will help you create rituals for the seasons in your life, which might not correspond to the season you are physically in right now. Feel free to do the ones that feel right for you in any given moment. With the exception of the Solstice and Equinox rituals that are for particular times of the year, most of the others can be used at any time.

Heartful Living

Whether we acknowledge the sacred daily or create once-in-a-lifetime rites of passage, the key to living a more sacred life is moving from our hearts. Our hearts are the center of life force in our physical bodies. The love in our spiritual hearts radiates from our souls and connects us to life.

∿ Heart Sounds ∿

In The Four Fold Way, *Angeles Arrien points out that dynamic, magnetic, and integrative life energies are found in all sacred music and are described by the three sounds ee, oh, and ah respectively. Shamanic and Gregorian chanting, vocalization of Judaic cantors, and Tibetan overtone sounds all work with these sounds to realign the three life forces.*

Since the heart is the place where all parts of ourselves come together, to me the heart represents the ah sound, or integrative energy. The heart is the place of unconditional love. In order for you to come from the heart when you speak and bring loved ones into the heart

when you listen, practice the ah sound for just a minute each morn-
ing. That way the spirit will live strongly in you.

All of us, men and women alike, have a lot in common as different hues of the same human family. We are all in bodies, and we eat, sleep, work, and carry on bodily functions in the same way. We all have had a mother and father. We need food, clothing, and shelter to survive. We are dependent on nature and are a part of nature. We require love, acknowl-edgement, and beauty to feed our souls. As unique drops of the great flowing river, we each require love, respect, and safety to be vulnerable and share from our hearts during transitions.

We also have differences that make us unique. No matter what your ethnic, cultural, or religious background, your personal experiences are important. Your career, marital status, sexual orientation, choices, cre-ative ventures, likes, and dislikes can endow your daily experience with the Divine with deep personal meaning. Our actions create a legacy for ourselves and loved ones whether we are conscious of it or not. We tell our personal story as we live it.

Through the suggestions that have worked for me and many others, may you feel supported in your sacred living. As you turn the pages of the book, let the experiences wash over and inspire you. Then listen to your heart. You will know what to do.

2

Ceremonies from the Heart

Only the symbolic life can express the need of the soul—the daily need of the soul mind you! And because people have no such thing, they can never step out of this mill—this awful grinding, banal life in which they are "nothing but." In the ritual, they are nearer the Godhead; they are even divine.

—Carl Jung

WHEN WE TAKE TIME TO CREATE a mean-ingful sacred event for ourselves, it is a self-loving action. We companion ourselves. We listen to our hearts and act on what is called for. When we include other people, isolation disap-pears as we share our personal stories—we have a purpose; we make a dif-ference; we feel loved and part of the world.

Rites of passage bring more awareness to our lives, simply by taking the time to do them. We need only to slow down and listen. So often when I have shared with people the rite of passage we performed for my nieces and nephews or how a family celebrated the arrival of their new-born, people comment that they thought of doing something similar but hadn't acted on it.

By acting on that fleeting thought, I want to honor my daughter's womanhood..., we shift relationship dynamics, everyone is informed of her change, denial of her growth and maturity disappears, and our family and friends take on different roles in the family group. Too often we let the next thought stop us, but I don't know how, and I don't have time. It takes courage to create something new. But we learn as we try.

A rite sets new boundaries and makes new connections at the same time. In a puberty ritual, for example, your daughter is honored and edu-cated about her budding maturity, and she is given new responsibility through the process of creating the rite with her. Everyone moves into more harmony with the flow of life's changes.

Our lives are full of important changes. Marriage, birth, and death are most commonly celebrated, because they are the transitions that traditionally carry the most impact on our lives. However by celebrating only these events, it becomes all too easy to speed our way through life without much thought to what happens in between. Celebrating life in between helps us to be more conscious of what we are doing here.

Besides the essentials of love, respect, trust, safety, and the knowledge that we are part of a greater whole, there are a few things that might assist you in composing rituals for yourself and your family. They have come from my personal observations of creating ceremonies over the last fifteen years and from the spiritual teachers I have studied with along the way.

Intention

The single most important element in any rite is setting your intention. Rituals are neutral containers of the present moment. You determine the positive or negative quality of that container and the flow of energy through the container by your attitude, frame of mind, and actions.

If you intend to honor yourself and others and support changes that are occurring in your life, your rite will be a positive experience. If you come with a negative frame of mind—resisting change, using the rite to control the outcome—the Universe will give you a negative experience. That's why clarity of intention is the most important element.

Simplicity

Keep it simple. If you find yourself creating a Broadway production, you may be missing the point. Return to what the ritual is about and use only the essentials. Complicated rites only distract you from the core meaning you intend to convey.

Take Your Time

Because you want to stay aware of what you are doing in the rite, it is important to go slowly. I like to imagine that I am entering a timeless dimension when I perform a ritual. In this space, there is nothing more important than what is happening right now. I unplug the phone, don't answer the door, make sure there is nothing else planned, and ask other participants to do the same. Most people instinctually know to do this. Occasionally, however, there are those so hooked into their schedules that they need permission to relax.

Know You Are Not Alone

It takes courage to create your first ritual, especially if you have never even attended one before. It's always scary to begin something new. That's part of the creative process. This book is designed to be a friend on the path, tested by others who have gone before you. All of the rites in this book have been tried by someone, and their experiences are here to guide you. It's normal to be afraid, and it's part of our evolution to go for it anyway.

We can choose to move through fear and not let it run our lives, knowing we are supporting internal growth and love.

Many times I have been afraid of looking silly or stupid. Sometimes I was afraid of not being able to speak the truth. What I have discovered is that people respond to your sincerity. They can feel your intention, as well as hear it. If you are coming from the heart, that is all you need.

Part of the fear of a ritual is facing the unknown. We don't always know how the Universe will create our new experiences. At some point, if we set our intention, come from our hearts, and do the ritual sincerely, the Universe responds in kind.

The most challenging thing is often letting go and trusting the process, which means dropping the need to control beyond what we are truly responsible for, then leaving enough room for spontaneity. It is intuition and spontaneity that make each rite unique, even if the format is the same every time.

Nature as Teacher

Every ritual throughout history has been based on nature. The four elements—Earth, Air, Fire, and Water—have been used in ritual to invoke blessings, remembrances, and to recount scripture or sacred stories. No matter where you live on the globe, there are the four elements and seven directions—north, east, south, west, as well as the Earth, sky, and the center—which all describe our place in the vast context of the natural world. Each element also relates to myriad aspects of human nature, which will be helpful to keep in mind when creating a ritual.

Various indigenous cultures use different colors for the four directions, for example. The differences depend on where they live, the terrain, the wind and weather patterns, seasonal fluctuations, and traditions they have learned from their families.

The Earth is often symbolized by the color green because it is said that Grandmother Earth heals all things. Indeed, all vitamins, minerals, and medications come originally from the Earth. Water is the life blood of the Earth. The Earth is considered feminine by Native American cultures, and Earth is considered the fifth direction.

The Sky is symbolized by the color blue. Grandfather Sky is the sustainer of life and includes the air we breathe, the stars we travel by, and the weather the brings rain. Sky is considered masculine and the sixth direction.

The center is where all the directions come together. It is the heart, unconditional love, the "I am," self-realization. It is the seventh direction.

In most Native American traditions, the Creator is neutral and loves all creations equally, no matter where you are on the wheel (north, east, south, west) or whether you are animal, mineral, or vegetable.

It is said that as we move through life, we move in a clockwise direction facing the center around the medicine wheel, from one direction to the other. In addition, each element contains positive and negative aspects. When we are in the north, or in our power, we face south, the direction of home, surrender, family, birth, and death. When we are in the east, the direction of new beginnings, we face west, the direction of the unknown. Thus we are reminded constantly of the apparent opposite of where we are, humbling us to the realities of life.

〜〜 Wings Riding with You 〜〜

Imagine that your guardian angel or spirit guide is walking or driving with you. Imagine their wings around your shoulders as your personal copilot, guiding you as you go.

When we are in transition, we are moving from one direction to the other. Rituals can reflect these changes by using one or more of the colors symbolizing a direction. For example, if you feel you are moving from the west or the unknown, represented by the color black, or into your power, or north, symbolized by the color white, you can use colored cloth on your body or on an altar.

Sometimes we move toward the center of the wheel where we can see everything spinning around us. This is a time when we feel powerful, present, soft, and strong—all at the same time. Then balance becomes the most critical focus. The Native Americans use a circle with the equidistant cross in the center to symbolize the four directions, Earth, sky, and the center.

The best reminder for creating rituals is found in Angeles Arrien's book, *The Four Fold Way.* She has researched many nature-based shamanic traditions throughout the world and describes four principles that can be found in virtually all traditions. These are four aspects of our inner nature in balance and harmony with the Universe. I find these extraordinary and use them to check my approach to life in creating rituals.

~~~ **Four Principles for Practicing Presence** ~~~

Show up and choose to be present. This allows us to access the human resources of power, presence, and communication.

Pay attention to what has heart and meaning. This opens us to the human resources of love, gratitude, acknowledgment, and validation.

Tell the truth without blame or judgment. Nonjudgmental truthfulness maintains our authenticity and develops our inner vision and intuition.

Be open to outcome, not attached to outcome. This help us recover the human resources of wisdom and objectivity.

Of course, no one can tell you how you should relate to the Universe or what has meaning for you. This is why these principals work so well. They ask us, without invoking guilt or shame, the question: "How am I being this moment?" They bring us back into harmony with the Universe and into our own experience.

Using Symbols

The symbols in a ritual can bring great personal significance to whatever you are doing. From your grandmother's wedding ring to your father's masonry pin, symbols can connect your historic roots and spiritual traditions with the present. They can establish an energy pattern during a rite and help you set your intention more firmly. I urge you to discover what has meaning for you and not to be afraid to use it because it may seem silly or too personal. What has meaning for you is what matters. If you choose not to use symbols, however, that is okay too. They are not necessary because the form you use is not as important as the clarity of intention—but they can be helpful in honing your intention.

～～ Sacred Symbols ～～

Here is an overview of the symbolism of various shapes, taken from my work, with the help of Angeles Arrien's book The Five Universal Shapes and How to Use Them:

Circle: Wholeness, completion, continuation, inclusion.

Oval: A sign of spirit, oval portraits of religious figures were often used throughout art history to represent the most divine beings.

Cross: The extended arms of a human, head at one end and legs together forming the other extension. They meet at the level of the heart, the center of all things. (As you may well know, the crucifix is an old Christian symbol. But its existence predates Christianity and is found throughout the world.)

Equidistant cross: Relationship, integration, and balanced connection. Found at the center of the Medicine Wheel and symbolizes the four directions, the four seasons, the four winds, the four corners of the Universe, and so forth.

Star of David: Two intersecting triangles coming together in the center forming a hexagram. The name David means beloved, so the Star of David is the star of the beloved. Triangles from Earth and the heavens meet in the heart center.

Five pointed star: *The shape is a human being with arms and legs extended.*

Medicine Wheel: *The symbol Native Americans use to express their wheel of life with the seven directions. A circle with an equidistant cross in the center of it.*

You may find yourself unable to avoid symbols: How you sit together, the patterns of dancing, the procession into or out of a space, the shape of the altar, or the elements used on it all play a part. Pay attention to what attracts you and the unfolding ceremony will teach you which symbols are personally important.

There are also universal shapes that have been used by people around the world that can affect the psychology of the rite as well as convey a deeper meaning. Whether people sit or stand in a room, in a circle, in rows, or in a square, the shape can affect one's sense of place and helps to shape the feeling of a rite. Straight rows of people facing a speaker, for example, lends itself to more authoritarian presentations. It also accommodates large groups of people. However, it is most natural for people to gather in a circle in family-sized groups. For centuries, we have gathered around campfires and sat in circles for storytelling and discussions. As for my own experience in circle gatherings—I feel part of the group and still an individual at the same time.

Be Aware of How You Pass Things Around

The direction that you pass things can also contribute to meaning. Johnny Moses, a Native American teacher on the northwest coast, says that prevailing winds have determined for various people the direction that they pass bowls, candles, cedar smoke or smudge, and so on. On his island, the prevailing winds move counterclockwise, so that is the direction that they pass objects. In other cultures, for example on the Great Plains, it is traditional to pass things clockwise, the same direction as the prevailing winds.

In most Earth-based traditions, the clockwise passing of ritual objects is affirmative, while counterclockwise supports dismantling or letting go. If you were releasing a part of your life—a job or emotions— passing things counterclockwise would support the letting go. However you may want to move things clockwise to affirm change, a new job, or other positive aspects of your life.

It doesn't matter which way you decide to pass objects, and it may depend entirely on the nature of the rite, the prevailing winds in your area, or what feels right at the time. What matters most is that your intention is clear and positive.

I suggest you choose which feels right to you and stick to it, unless you intend to intentionally shift for a specific purpose. Consistency helps set your overall intention more firmly, and you won't have to reestablish your groundwork every time.

Beginnings, Middles, and Endings

Our life stories are the experiences that form us, help us grow, and give meaning to our life. They are important. A rite becomes a segment of your personal story. It can gather parts of your past together in conclusion to move to the next step in your future. That's why a rite should have a beginning, middle, and end—just like your life.

In his book *The Rites of Passage*, Arnold Van Gennep defined the beginning of a rite as separation, the middle as transition, and the end as incorporation. Here is the core of his ideas.

During a ritual, various segments can be emphasized depending on the nature of the ceremony. For example, in an adolescent rite, separation may constitute the initial phase, while transition and incorporation take place during the majority of the ritual. A funeral may emphasis separation and transition, while incorporation may be dealt with at the end of the funeral in the form of prayers or offerings for the soul of the deceased, then may extend into the grieving process.

Parties, Celebrations, Ceremonies, and Rituals

For clarity, here are some definitions. Parties and celebrations are basically the same thing. A gathering of people having a good time. Celebrations can be for an entire city, while parties are generally smaller. Rituals can be a segment of the party, or they can be the whole event, if it is thought of in the context of marking a transition. A ceremony is a ritual, although not necessarily spiritual in nature, such as an awards ceremony. In this book you can make the assumption that I am always speaking of a spiritual context, therefore I use ceremony and ritual interchangeably.

A ritual draws this distinction; it is a point in time when we consciously make a transition from one way of life to another. It can be fun or not; it holds all possibilities; it is not necessarily a party or a celebration, but it can be, just as parties and celebrations can be rituals if the intention is stated as such, and the actions are carried out to correspond with the intention.

Rituals can be fun as well as meaningful. Spontaneity and humor can be as much a part of a rite as anything. Some of my favorite rites are centered around a meal where humor is part of the fabric of the celebration. As long as you don't lose focus for long, humor can bond and heal people. A great deal depends on the attitude of those leading the event and how they set the tone for other participants.

3

Daily Practice

*Let us live in peace and harmony to keep the
land and all life in balance. Only prayer and
meditation can do that.*

—Thomas Banyacya, Hopi Elder

WHETHER WE ADMIT IT OR NOT, the world is a miraculous place. Every day we are given the gift of awareness of those miracles and the free choice to notice them or not. The simple act of breathing; opening your hand; and watching others move, play, talk, or smile can transform our day if we let it.

Daily spiritual practice is the best way to set the tone for each precious day and cultivate an inner observer who remains neutral to our dramas and challenges. By developing an inner observer, we can gain an understanding of our patterns and tendencies and can participate in life with an awareness that we are. We do this by creating space inside to simply experience ourselves. That's what it means to have an inner life.

There are many ways to do this, the simplest and most direct are prayer and meditation. They are two parts of a conversation with what is all around us and within us—a call and response. Prayer is asking for what we need; meditation (or contemplation) is listening for the answer. By practicing both, you develop a relationship to that which lives in us.

Of course, whatever you call that which gives us life is up to you. There are many names for the Great Mystery—Nature, the Divine, Krishna, the Earth, the Universe, God, Goddess, to name a few. It is paramount to have daily conversations with ourselves regarding what is living in us. For if we are not in touch with our primary source, what else gives us meaning in life?

Every great religion has a form of contemplation and a form of prayer that helps in daily spiritual practice. Some religions do not teach meditation actively, such as Christianity. Yet, in Christian religious orders, there are methods of meditation that are taught to the novitiates. Other religions regularly teach meditation, such as Buddhism. Others use chanting or cantering as a form of conversation with God.

In Earth-based cultures, meditation is not taught per se, but listening to nature is. In many Native American traditions, the vision quest could be considered a form of meditation that is performed all at once—over one, two, four, or seven days. Tracking is another form of meditation, specifically walking meditation.

Many people today who are not part of a conventional religion still feel they have a spiritual life. However you define that relationship, it is *yours* to create and sustain.

～～ Your Personal Altar ～～

An altar is a wonderful focal point for your daily practice. Altars are simple to construct. You can use a scarf in the center of the floor, or take a box, small table, or chair and cover it with one or all of the colors of the four directions, for example. Place something meaningful to you in the center, a ring, a photo, a book, or whatever works for you. You can also create group altars. Sharing the meaning of what you are placing on the altar helps to bond the group and deepen the experience for everyone.

Meditation

Meditation is the oldest and best way to become aware of both our inner life and the life around us. The most common form of meditation is to sit quietly in a chair or on the floor with your back supported and count your inhalations and exhalations. This does not mean you hyperventilate. You simply concentrate on your ordinary breathing, and count to ten. When you reach ten start over again at one. If you do not reach ten without being distracted, do not chastise yourself—just begin again at one. Notice that you have drifted and lovingly and gently bring yourself back to one.

While this sounds easy enough, you may find that it is more difficult than you anticipated. Just remember that, as Carlos Canstenada said in Journey to Xilan, "The spiritual warrior is always at the beginning." If you have to begin again, no matter, just stay with it. Sitting for fifteen or twenty minutes is a good beginning. Take your time. Do not rush.

The most difficult thing for most people is to find the time to meditate. But if you give yourself this gift, you will find your life runs more smoothly. You begin to notice life more instead of reacting to it. Each time you meditate, whether once or twice a day (morning and evening), the process acts as a link in a chain of inner strength, becoming your guideline to a spiritual life. Especially when things are most turbulent, meditation brings you to that inner wellspring of peace that lives in your heart.

Of course, if you haven't paid much attention to the well in the past, you may have to clear it out first! Try to notice what thoughts and feelings come up that may be clogging your harmony. Just remember: They are thoughts and feelings, nothing more. You do not need to give them power, just notice that they arise and pass away. Your persistent presence, your observer, will restore you to balance.

In each season, I suggest several meditations. These will give you a sense of the inner aspects of an outer action. They are meant to inspire you to find what is right for you. By all means, if you need a "winter warrior meditation" in mid-summer, use it!

I have found that my meditation practice has changed over the years and continues to change constantly. I began with a mantra given to me through transcendental meditation, which then evolved into breathing, walking sometimes, and being still and feeling life living in me. Creating (writing, playing music, art, theater, singing) is also a form of meditation for me.

～～ Other Forms of Meditation ～～

There are also walking meditations, such as counting your breaths as you step, and mantras or sacred names that are repeated over and over, singing, chanting, or just sitting and being still for a period of time. There are numerous books on meditation, which describe each of these forms, available at your library or bookstore. Some sources are listed in the bibliography.

Meditation is the most important time of the day for me. I do it first thing in the morning, which aligns me and sets me on a positive course.

I also meditate during the day if need be. Over the years, I have developed an inner home, a place of inner peace that I can come back to again and again.

Prayer

Another important tool for daily spiritual practice is prayer. Prayer is simply asking for what we want and then believing that what was asked for will come. It requires a request and then a letting go to allow the Spirit to bring you an answer. The answer does not usually come in the way you thought, however, and the timing is definitely not up to you, (although you can ask for divine timing, the best possible outcome, and a number of other requests that set everything in the right flow).

In my experience, prayer is not bartering or pleading with the Spirit. That does not seem to work very well. What does work is to be humble, direct, and not to manipulate the outcome. Prayer is knowing what we want, what is needed, and asking for that. At the same time, however, it is an acknowledgment that we are not in control of the process of life.

Praying for others is sometimes tricky. Some religions teach that we should pray only for others. Other religions say to pray only for your needs and for the health of others. In my experience, praying for another's clarity of guidance and the best outcome is often enough. We can never know what the best outcome is for another, nor, in my opinion, should we interfere in their process (including their dying process—the most loving thing we can do sometimes is to let go of those we love, knowing they have their own road to travel).

~~~ **Prayer for Any Day** ~~~

I pray for the best outcome for _____ . May you help her find peace, joy, and more love. I pray for his good health and that he may find the help he needs. Thank you for my life. Help my lessons come easily and with gentleness. Help me to hear what I need to hear and to see the things I need to see for my highest and wisest good. May it be so. Blessed be.

Creating Rites of Menses

During women's monthly flow, resting and renewal have been practiced in many indigenous cultures. Secret rites of womanhood, which included initiating women into their roles and responsibilities as mothers, wives, and food gatherers, as well as initiating them into the sacred knowledge of the body, were the primary purposes of these rites.

Today we have nearly lost connection with the sacred nature of our bodies. Reframing the negative messages into positive ones takes vigilant observation of what we tell ourselves as well as societal messages we accept as true. Creating monthly rites, however simple, will help us remember how beautiful and sacred a vessel our bodies are.

You can do this alone or in groups. When several women together meet on a monthly basis, you can create a support system that helps everyone. If you have children, especially teenage girls, give them support and blessing during their monthly flow through a rite. It helps them grow up with a better self-image. Here are some suggestions:

1. Schedule time for yourself during the full moon or during the first day(s) of your monthly flow.

2. Take a private area of the house, the top of a dresser or book-case, or a shelf of a closet and create an altar there. Let your family know it is a place for you and no one else, unless you choose to share it.

3. Set things on it that are important to you and use it as a place of focus for prayer and meditation. It can also be a room, like an artist's studio for exploring creative ideas. Let yourself create pictures, poems, a journal, or just go there to sing.

4. Make a commitment to yourself to take time out.

5. For a moontime support group, talk to other women. You don't need many women, three or four will do. If you need help, refer to Starhawk's *The Spiral Dance*, my book, *Dancing Up the Moon*, or Zsuzsanna Budapest's *The Holy Book of Women's Mysteries*.

    a. Make a commitment to meet every month.

    b. Pass the leadership from person to person so no one feels overburdened. You can also make it a leaderless group, with one person per month focusing the activities and discussion.

    c. The leader can bring something specific to share or can choose an activity or a topic for discussion. Here are some suggestions: drum together (drums are the heartbeat of the

Earth; they can transform your mood and temperament); create rites together to transform and heal each other during difficult times; give each other massages (it's a great way to bond and help one another relax); pass around a talking stick and use the group to tell how you really feel in the moment; and brainstorm together about what you each want from the group.

d. Create rites of passage for yourself or for your daughters that will positively affirm womanhood.

e. Dream together of how different our planet would be if every group of women had their own moon circle.

～～ Heartful Presence ～～

Sit quietly and place your hand on your heart and close your eyes. Let yourself breathe very deeply and notice that your heart is beating. It is alive, beating without your having to do anything. Consider circulation: Imagine your blood being reoxegenated and filtered as you breathe Be with your miraculous being.

Walking with the Spirit

All forms of spiritual practice are to help you live in the awareness of the mystery that surrounds us, every moment. Brian Swimme, Ph.D., who is a cosmologist and one of my spiritual teachers, says that for him, spiritual practice is about increasing those "cosmic moments of connectedness," until our lives become filled with awe and joy for living.

I would say it a little differently. The more we practice noticing life, the more we notice that life is noticing our noticing! Then we are in relationship with the Spirit. We are never alone; we feel a part of everything around us no matter where we go. We naturally develop more love, respect, and trust in the Universe. We are part of something wonderful here on planet Earth, something awesome, something beyond words.

When we practice walking with the Spirit, we are simply moving through our day with the knowledge that we are loved by this mystery that is all around us. Walking with the Spirit is staying in love with our lives and knowing that we are loved.

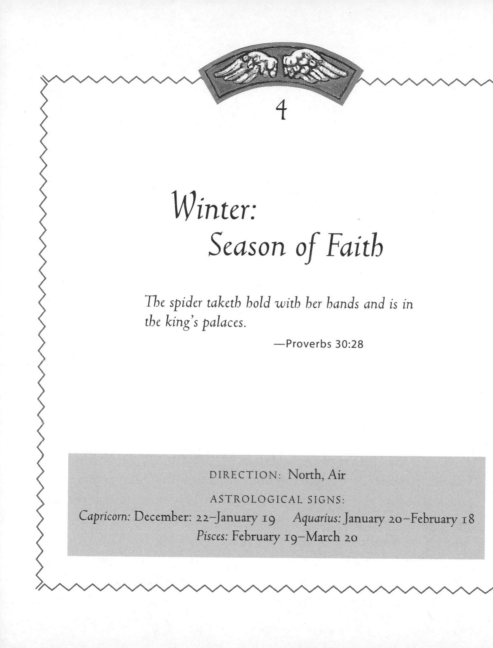

4

Winter:
Season of Faith

The spider taketh hold with her hands and is in the king's palaces.

—Proverbs 30:28

DIRECTION: North, Air

ASTROLOGICAL SIGNS:

Capricorn: December: 22–January 19   *Aquarius:* January 20–February 18

Pisces: February 19–March 20

WINTER, WITH ITS LONG DARK NIGHTS, is the time of year that we celebrate the light at the heart of darkness. For this reason, winter is known as the season of faith. That's why lighting candles and filling our homes with twinkling lights are major symbols for this time.

From December 21, the first day of winter, into March, winter is the season of rest, the period of going inside the house and inside ourselves. In the animal and plant world, it is a time of dormancy, of hibernation. Winter offers an opportunity to envision the new year with those sparks of inspiration that come to us in the darkness. Thus it is a strongly interior season, not only because the days are shorter, but because winter is silent. Silence is required for us to hear the call of the new.

Many people around the world believe that the year really begins during the darkness of the winter solstice. It makes sense because we all begin our journey on Earth in the dark womb of our mothers.

Contrary to the natural rhythms of the Earth and the dormancy of our hemisphere, our culture makes this season the busiest time of the year, when we get together with friends and family, travel across the country, and enjoy holiday parties. Although such celebrations are important, be sure to take some contemplative time for yourself.

That's why I have included here celebrations, rites, and suggestions to help you get in touch with your inner self, as well as ways to celebrate with the outside world. Of course the outer activities affect us inwardly, and the inner changes shift our perception of the outer world, so one is always interacting with the other.

Weatherwise, the months of January, February, and March are the most challenging. We are pressed against the reality of our survival more radically than at other times of the year. It is also a time when we seem to lose elders to disease or old age. That's why in this section on winter I have also included information on rites of death, disease, and letting go.

This is the time to find inner strength and resolve, for it can be a challenging time, one in which our faith is tested. It's important to gather personal power and inward strength now. According to Angeles Arrien, there are three kinds of power for us to consider: presence, communication, and position. The first is the power of awareness of ourselves and that which lives around us. It is our vibrational tone, our harmonic resonance, our witness-self. The second is the power of our voice, how well we communicate what we feel, think, and know. The latter is synonymous with service and responsibility and asks us to look at how we use our position to serve and create.

〰️ Symbols and Key Words for Winter 〰️

Spiral, tree of life, evergreen, holly, mistletoe, candles, lights, mind, intelligence, power, the ethereal, life force, invisible presence, air, spirit, the color white, cold. Consider the source of storms. An empty bowl or white cloth can be used to symbolize this direction.

DECEMBER 21, **Winter Solstice, Light.** *I light my way with love.*

Winter solstice is a time to rest in your faith that through the darkness of winter the sun will return. Around the world it is a time of the festival of light; in Mexico, Sweden, Norway, Australia, and throughout Europe, it is a time to honor the light that is found within every soul.

～～ Winter Equinox Celebration ～～

At night or as the sun sets, by yourself or in a small group, sit in a circle with a candle or a fire in the middle. Imagine that the flame or flames extend out around you and now centers itself within your own heart. Sound the oh sound together (you may also find that you naturally sound the ancient name for God: aum (pronounced om). Make the sound three times resonating with your heart center. Then let yourself fall into silence. Stay in the silence for as long as you need to be there. Then open yourself to receive whatever you may.

When you feel complete, you may or may not want share your experiences. Imagine that the flame comes back to the center flame and remains in your heart. You may want to say something like "Now the light is back in the center of our hearts and the center of our circle. All is well."

Perhaps you can share food together. Let the candle burn down.

DECEMBER 22, **Harmony.** *The love inside me harmonizes my being.*

Try to walk with the flame inside you all day today. Whether you are at work, at home, or at play, let yourself feel that you are living, flourishing in the darkest time of the year. Imagine a tone coming from the flame.

DECEMBER 23, **Tree of Life.** *My body is the tree of life, I honor its strengths and weaknesses, which give me signals around which I can grow.*

The tree is a powerful symbol for life. This is why so many people are drawn to having a tree in their homes, whether there are Christian cele-brations or not. The lights of a Christmas tree represent bringing the light out of the darkness. Originally a pagan celebration of the tree of life, this ritual has deep significance for anyone drawn to its symbolism.

Conflict Resolution

The joy of the holidays is often accompanied with unfinished conflicts within families. Here is an idea for those holiday gatherings you love to hate. All of us have two choices for the holidays: We can choose to spend them somewhere else, or we can clear up the issues and enjoy the holi-days in more love and harmony together. Yes, I know, easier said than done, but it is possible.

First discuss with your family (or other group) that your intent is to clear up unfinished business among you. Name the issues and discuss directly with the people involved what you would like to do. Remember conflict is not all you may want to express. You can share tender unex-pressed loving feelings too. Tell them you have found a way that might work if people are open to trying something new, because you can't heal a problem by doing the same old thing.

Use a talking stick. When a person has the stick, no one else is allowed to speak. The person with the stick can say anything and everything that's on his or her mind, as long as they *speak from the heart and with respect*.

When expressing yourself, try to avoid the word *but*. It tends to cancel what you have said previously. *And*, on the other hand, is inclusive. Also, try to speak in *I* statements as much as possible, such as *I feel* or *I need*.

It is a good idea to make this stick together, a project that could be done by the boys or men in the family. Everyone should contribute something of themselves to this stick. That way they have invested their energy into it. It can be elaborate or a simple stick, with carving or beads, jewelry, or stones glued to it.

Any object designating a spokesperson, such as a stone, a small sculpture, or staff, will create the same result. I know of a men's group in Atlanta that uses a black onyx egg signifying the deep tender feelings that men have buried. If you use a stone or something that does not need embellishment, pass it around the room in the circle of your relatives as you begin and ask that as they hold it, they state their intention for the gathering. For example, "I, Jasmine, intend to do my part to restore love and harmony and share my truth in this family." Of course each person will have their own words.

The talking stick or stone does several important things. First, it restores a sense of respect among those engaged in conflict. Secondly, it gives each family member the opportunity to be heard without interruption. This is especially important with children.

I have adopted its use in youth groups, sharing feelings and good-byes for graduating high school seniors, with friends and family members during times of parting, and at other times when events or feelings need to be discussed. It can be used to honor someone leaving for school, for work abroad, or to share deep and tender feelings when it is hard to say something. If you move from the heart, tell the truth, and remain respectful, your conflicts may turn into compassion, love, and better understanding.

〜〜 Ancient Wisdom for Today 〜〜

The idea of the talking stick has been widely used by Native Americans for centuries. In some African tribes, such as the Dogon, a spokesman carries a staff, which designates him to have the power to announce the king or chief's proclamations. Although in Africa the stick is not passed around from person to person, the idea of designating someone to speak by way of a stick is similar.

DECEMBER 24, **Christmas Eve, Gift.** *I pause to reflect on the unseen gifts that I already possess.*

In many European countries, especially Scandinavia, Norway, Sweden, and Denmark, this day marks the Christmas celebration. Gifts are opened on this night instead of Christmas morning, and there are special foods prepared, such as gelatinous, lye-soaked cod called *lutefisk* and potato bread that looks like large tortillas called *lefse*.

People from all over the world attend Christmas Eve Candlelight Service at midnight to herald the birth of the Christ Child. Many people today also celebrate it as the birth of the light of consciousness within humanity.

〜〜 A Christmas Bath 〜〜

Burn frankincense in your bathroom when taking a winter soak. This fragrant resin from a tree grown only in Saudi Arabia has been used for centuries as a sacred aromatic. It is used in aromatherapy to ben-efit the skin, as a nerve sedative, for cell rejuvenation, and as an anti-inflammatory. Frankincense and myrrh were given to Mary and Joseph in honor of Jesus' birth. At the time, frankincense was more valuable than gold.

Light a candle and turn off the lights. In an incense burner that holds a piece of charcoal, burn the frankincense. This would be espe-cially great after skiing, sledding, or skating.

DECEMBER 25, **Christmas Day, Giving and Receiving.** *I allow myself to receive by giving and give by receiving.*

Originally the birth of the fiery sun god Mythras, Christmas is the day celebrated as the birth of the Son of God. Today, take a few moments to contemplate the birth of the light within yourself as well as the birth of the historic Jesus.

DECEMBER 26, **Unity**. *I gather with my loved ones to join together in unity and wholeness.*

Kwanzaa, a Swahili word meaning first as in First Fruits, was an end of the year celebration designed for African Americans by Professor Maulana Karenga of the Black Studies Department at California State University Long Beach in 1966. It is a feast of lights with symbols such as a straw mat or *mkeka*, a candle holder or *kinara*, and seven candles *(mshumaa saba)* of red, black, and green, which represent the spilled blood of ancestors, the celebrants' black skin, and the green of good land. According to the *World Holiday Book*, the mshumaa sabe are lit from December 26 until the first of the year. The candles are lit for the seven sacred principles: *umoja*, unity; *kujichagulia*, self-determination; *umija*, collective action; *ujamaa*, cooperative economics; *nia*, purpose; *kuumba*, creativity; and *imani*, faith.

Each night, families read from books on the lives of historic figures who exemplify these principles. Meals are prepared and recipes are taken from South America, the Caribbean, the American South, Africa, and elsewhere. Kwanzaa has become very popular among many African Americans.

DECEMBER 27, **Self-Determination**. *I release the gathering of the last few days and stand in the power of self-love, knowing what is right for me today.*

DECEMBER 28, **Collective Action.** *I stand shoulder to shoulder with my family, whether they be spiritual or in physical body, to take corrective action in the community.*

DECEMBER 29, **Cooperative Economics.** *Money is energy and commitment. I invest in my well-being by sharing with my community.*

DECEMBER 30, **Purpose.** *Through my purpose, being fully who I am, I acknowledge all aspects of my being and share what is constructive with others.*

DECEMBER 31, **Creativity.** *I express my creativity freely and encourage creative expression in those around me.*

New Year's Eve Ideas

Many cities now celebrate First Night, annual community celebrations on New Year's Eve. For example, in Boston, there is a series of musical events. In Santa Cruz during First Night, folks construct a giant Phoenix out of chicken wire, then offer people on the streets a chance to write down their wishes for the new year on a fiery "feather" (piece of paper) and tie it to the mythical bird. The feathers are kept on the bird until the following year when they are burned and new feathers are made. This would be a great neighborhood or family idea as well.

Although many people choose to celebrate New Year's Eve with champagne and parties, some choose a quieter time. Here are some alternatives to the New Year's Eve bash: Spend New Year's Eve alone—chanting, praying, or reciting the many names of God; spend time this night in retreat with a few close friends, declaring good intentions for the coming year; spend the evening with one good friend or your spouse using a divination tool, such as the runes or tarot to set the tone for the new year.

〰〰 New Year's Eve Burning Bowl Ritual 〰〰

Practiced in the Unity Church every year, this ritual helps people release the old and gather the new. Write down what you are releasing from the year past—these can be old relationships, habits, or ways of being, for example. Then release the paper into a lit fireplace or a brass bowl, setting the paper aflame. You may want to lay the fire very carefully, letting yourself put your full awareness into its arrangement. When you are finished, write down what you want to keep or renew, then tuck it in your pocket. This can include qualities of trust, harmony, balance, hope, abundance, more love, a new home, or better job—whatever you choose.

January

Knowing others is intelligence;
knowing yourself is true wisdom.
Mastering others is strength;
mastering yourself is true power.

—Lao-tzu

THE MONTH OF JANUARY IS NAMED after the Roman god Janus, the two-headed god of gateways. The Latin root is *janua*, which means gate. His female equivalent is the goddess Juno-Janus, who looks with her two heads simultaneously forward and backward. The Aztecs have many two-headed gods, the most famous of whom is Quetzacotal, the plumed serpent with heads of a man and a woman. The Nordic people named the month after their primary god, Thor. The Anglo-Saxons and Early-Americans called January Wolf Moon because it was the time of year when the wolves came into the village to look for food. It is also called the Snow Moon because it is the coldest month of the year in the northern hemisphere. Symbols for the month are the snow drop, carnation, and garnet.

January is a good time to bring ourselves face-to-face with our personal plans. This is the time to assess the past year and make resolutions for the new year—start new exercise programs, or put our homes in order for the activities of the coming year. That's why, during January, I have included many cleansing, clearing, and purification rites.

JANUARY 1, **Faith.** *I step into the new year with faith, for the love and joy I share.*

New Year's Day heralds much bell ringing, from Japan to Bulgaria, as people ring out the old and ring in the new. It is a good day for purification after New Year's Eve, if drinking spirits was your way to celebrate. Before you feast on New Years Day with family or friends, let someone ring a bell, perhaps the youngest child or the youngest person present. She can say something simple like "Welcome new year, we are glad you are here."

～～ Dance Your Way into the New Year! ～～

Make yourself a rattle from a dried gourd. Take time to discover what symbols might be important to you and paint them on the rattle. Then use the rattle in your January meditation. The standing meditation for January is to dance in place with the intention of building strength of your presence in your work, your life, and throughout your day, while shaking your rattle.

Focus your mind and hold the intention clearly, while saying, "I intend to integrate the energies _____ and _____ in the New Year," or some such intention of your own making.

JANUARY 2, **Integration.** *I integrate plans and activities for the new year with ease and joy.*

One of the best ways to integrate energy is to dance. You can use drums, rattles, instruments, or just put on your favorite tunes that will help you dance your way into the new year. You can invite people over, or go out on the town. Either way if you set your intention on integration, just watch your plans take form!

JANUARY 3, **Purification.** *I stand in the shower of purifying golden light love and peace to begin my new year with ease.*

With the exception of baptism, there are no rituals that I know of in our culture that address purification. As a form of renewal to mark beginnings, a purification ritual is important to do at this time of the year.

In many tribal traditions, purification for both men and women is part of monthly moon cycles. In the Native American tradition, sweat lodges, like the original Scandinavian saunas, purify the body. Although saunas are used today for cleansing and recreation, the sweat lodge is a ceremony and usually takes place once a month, during the spring and fall equinox, or during the summer and winter solstice. Because what makes a ceremony is the use of intention before, during, and in closing any activity, if you have access to a sauna, you can make it sacred by intending to use it in a purifying spiritual, emotional, physical, or mental manner.

Smoke from burning small sage or cedar boughs is used before many indigenous Native American ceremonies. The sage cleanses the air and the cedar is thought to call forth positive energy. The process is called smudging. In India, incense is used to purify the air. It also sets the mood for meditation and deeper communion with the Spirit.

For me, purification has become a necessary part of my spiritual practice. Whether I partake in monthly sweat lodges, annual spring retreats, or simply smudge myself or my house from time to time, I always feel renewed and ready to begin again.

〰〰 A Releasing January Bath 〰〰

The Complete Guide to Aromatherapy suggests the following: one drop of lavender oil, two drops of rosemary, one drop of peppermint, and three drops of thyme in a warm bath. Lavender cleanses, peppermint rejuvenates and stimulates, rosemary cleanses the liver and helps ease nerves, and thyme treats mental fatigue as well as a number of other problems. Do not use rosemary or thyme, however, if you are pregnant because each can act as an abortive agent.

Seven-Day Ritual for the New Year, January 4–10

Before you go to sleep for the next seven nights, practice this ritual to help you get your life in order for the coming year. Simply follow the directions for each day. Each step is part of the ritual. At the end, you will have a new view of your life. In a journal, take note of what your soul is saying during these seven days. Watch your dreams and record them before you get out of bed, by having your journal and a pen near your pillow.

JANUARY 4, **Action.** *I can take action in my life that sets my course for the coming year. All is well.*

Set your intention for the new year. You can intend more love, harmony, peace, abundance, greater awareness, or whatever you choose. Write it down and make it a clear simple statement.

JANUARY 5, **Gratitude.** *I am grateful for the lessons in my life.*

Make a gratitude list. Take as much paper as you need. Your rite can begin here—acknowledging those friends, family, and coworkers who have supported you.

JANUARY 6, **Lessons.** *I acknowledge and release my lessons of the past and open to my lessons for the coming year.*

Reflect on your life story, listing the top ten events and circumstances that have brought you thus far. List your regrets and sorrows on one list and lessons learned and successes on the other. Congratulate yourself for each lesson and success.

JANUARY 7 AND 8, **Forgiveness.** *In order to go forward in peace and harmony, I forgive myself for the past and for my shortcomings. I forgive others for their actions and shortcomings too.*

Take your regrets and sorrows list from January 6. Next to it, write "I forgive myself," or "I forgive this person," for each one listed. If you can't do it, circle it. Then make a second list of actions you may need to take to clear up those regrets or sorrows. These may be people you need to forgive, ways of being that don't work anymore, or wounds in your past that need to be released. Read the list of what you want, release, then take the appropriate actions to forgive, confront, or speak to those people. When you are complete, and only when you feel complete, burn the list.

JANUARY 9, **Quality**. *I honor the qualities I have and the lessons that have shown me what I value.*

Ask yourself, "What qualities, such as patience, compassion, forgiveness, and so on, do I want to develop more fully?" Who are the people who exemplify these qualities to you? You can use water, essential oils, perfume, or ash from the burned release list to adorn and bless yourself with each new quality.

JANUARY 10, **Surrender**. *My prayers for the coming year are released to my highest good and rest in the Creator's hands.*

Take your list of qualities and read it again, then take your list of successes and lessons learned and end your seven-day ritual with this prayer, "This or something better, whatever is for my highest good." This sets your intention for right action, surrender, and the best possible outcome.

～～ Dream On! ～～

There are many books on dreams; one I can recommend is Jeremy Taylor's book Dreamwork, *which gives ways to record and interpret your dreams. Here are some clues to dreams. which he suggests might be helpful. Recording your dreams is easy. One suggestion is to keep*

*a dream notebook or journal with a pen near your bedside. Another
suggestion is to title your dream just as soon as you awaken. This
will help you remember the major images without losing the essence.
Some people keep a small tape recorder; this way you can just begin
to describe your dream.*

JANUARY 11, **Dreams.** *I honor the images of my dreams. They inform me of
the growth cycle I am in.*

Keeping a dream journal is a great way to create an understanding of
where you are in your inner life. The inner informs the outer and vice
versa. Some dreams we don't forget because we cannot understand their
meaning and symbols right away—some have to unfold over time for
us. Sometimes it isn't until we live the dream that its meaning is
revealed. If your dream strikes you as an initiation dream, something
very informative for your soul growth, it is especially important to
record it.

Creating a Rite from a Dream

1. Try to distinguish the most powerful images in the dream. They will
   be the key that will unlock the new feeling tone that you may have
   and will help you create the actual ritual. By feeling tone I mean the
   sense of awareness or shift in your inner knowing, a realization or
   "aha" that you might have come across as a result of your dream.

2. Think of the dream as a story that you wish to write. Play with it and don't be concerned if you have never done this before. This is not a Broadway production; it is a private play for you and a few others, who you may wish to invite. Perhaps writing a play or a story is not your medium. Try a song, dance the new you, or simply invite some friends over to hear a poem you have written about such a dream. Remember, this is your rite, and you can create it anyway you choose. So long as your intention is to heal your spirit, there can be nothing that should stop you from going for it.

3. Set the date and time for the rite, and tell those whom you want to invite. This is very important. Committing to a day helps you to carry out the plan.

4. Invite your guests. They can be important witnesses for you to make the shift. It also helps those friends or family closest to you to understand how you have changed. If they have questions about what you're doing, have them read this. It may help them to create a rite of their own.

5. It may take you a few days to create the ritual, so take your time. Let it unfold; you will be amazed at what transpires.

～～ Eye Pillow ～～

Rest your eyes for those long mid-winter sleeps with this eye pillow. Take a piece of cotton or silk cloth eight inches long and five inches wide. Fold it in half the long way, and, with the front sides together, sew it on two sides, leaving one narrow end open. Cut the seams close to the stitching and fold right side out, so that the sewn seams are inside. Fill with rice, leaving enough space so that the eye pillow will lay easily over the contours of your eyes and nose. Fold edges of the open side inward, then stitch closed. Sleep with the eye pillow over your eyes and rest well!

JANUARY 1 2, **Courage.** *I see myself through loving and accepting eyes.*

It takes courage to look at yourself honestly and to tell the truth about how you feel in your life. Take the time to be with those feelings after your seven-day ritual. Give yourself support and acknowledge yourself for the courage you have shown in your life.

JANUARY 1 3, **Faith.** *My faith lights my way beyond appearances. I rest in my sense of knowing.*

Imagine your faith in life as a light placed inside your heart long ago. It is glowing there, and as you focus on your light, imagine that it is growing brighter and brighter. That it is as large as your chest, as large as your body, and then as large as your outer field (about three feet around you). Let it glow steadily, surely; just allow faith to be.

JANUARY 1 4, **Inspiration.** *I allow inspiration to spark my life force and ignite a child's sense of play.*

Look around at your life. What is it that inspires you? If nothing comes to mind, ask yourself what last made you feel inspired. How did that feel? Allow that to reenter your experience now. Remember what it was that gave you a sense of wonder and awe. Imagine for a moment how you could continue to allow that spark of inspiration improve your life today.

JANUARY 15, **Bridging.** *I am making a bridge today, acknowledging myself, acknowledging others through my day.*

Meditation for Martin Luther King, Jr.'s Birthday

While Martin Luther King, Jr.'s birthday has become a secular holiday, for many it is a spiritual holiday as well. Everyone knows what this man accomplished during his lifetime. As a spiritual leader, he crossed boundaries of race and religion to bring people of different backgrounds together. Why not use the occasion to recommit to unity, harmony, and balance on the Earth.

Light a candle and let its light radiate and shine around you.(I choose four candles: black, white, red, and yellow for the four races.) Sit quietly with yourself, friends, or family and ask the question: "How can I bring more peace to my life in all areas? In my mind, . . . in my heart . . . in my body . . . , in my emotions . . . How can I bring more harmony between people? How can I join forces with all things, people, and places to bring this about?"

Then go into your heart for a moment and find the peace within. Imagine a garden or a wild place inside you. You might imagine a master, your higher self, Martin Luther King, Jr., or a spiritual teacher there assisting you. Know that his or her presence within is an aspect of you. Then fill your entire being with his or her light and healing. Feel it start in your heart and radiate out from your center. Let it radiate out from you and your circle and let it expand out to your group, throughout the house, the neighborhood, your city, state, the country, the world, around the world. When you are complete, bring your energy back into your own heart, offering thanks and gratitude. Let yourself feel the healing. All is well.

JANUARY 16, **Acknowledge.** *I acknowledge everyone's source of divine guidance and good intention.*

JANUARY 17, **Respect.** *I respect myself on every level for my presence in the world.*

JANUARY 18, **Presence.** *With my gift of presence, I support healing in the world.*

JANUARY 19, **Harmony.** *I resonate every cell with harmony.*

JANUARY 20, **Joy.** *The feelings of joy bubble in my heart.*

JANUARY 21, **Trust.** *Today I let go of that which I cannot control and trust that I am supported by the Spirit.*

We trust the air to support us without even thinking and the Earth to support us with every step. We trust fire and heat to cook our food. Imagine trusting the water enough to float—water being symbolic of our emotions. Imagine that we can expand our trust to the Earth and all that lives around us and through us.

Rite Before Surgery
Following on the theme of winter, a time to let go and release, is a ceremony for surgery that can assist anyone through an illness.

There are many ways to perform a ritual before surgery. Many procedures are done early in the morning, and the patient arrives at the hospital a few hours before. That's why it may work best to do a ritual the night before at home with family or friends.

Call a gathering of friends and family before your surgery to pray for the best outcome. You may want to pass the talking stick as a way to share feelings openly. You may need to invite only those who will help the patient relax and stay calm.

Have the person facing surgery sit in the center of a circle with unlit votive candles in front of him, if he is able. Each person coming to the ritual brings something that symbolizes a quality, like patience (maybe a stone), healing (perhaps a scarf blessed by friends and family), or strength, which helped them through a tough time. You can also pass a stone, having each person write their quality in it, so the patient can take it to the hospital with them.

One after another, each person gives his or her gift to the person in the center, telling the story of the object and or a story from their life describing an ordeal. They can begin with the words, "I give you the gift of. . ." The person in the center, receiving the gift, says, "I accept the gift of patience (strength, healing, and so on) from you and give you light." She or he then lights a candle in front of him and hands it to the person who just gave the gift.

The rite continues until everyone has had a turn, and the person in the center of the circle is surrounded by friends and candles. You can blow them out or let them burn down. The candles can also go with each one of the participants to be lit again on the day of the procedure to focus energy or to pray for the person having surgery. Group hugs are often a great way to end any rite.

To avoid any last-minute complications, it would be best to discuss any prayers that you might want to say in the operating room with your doctor before you enter the hospital because it would be unusual to spontaneously create something right in the operating room. Most doctors would not be opposed to pausing a moment before a procedure and saying a few words of blessing, but it would be best to check ahead of time with your particular doctor.

If the idea of prayer is uncomfortable to you, ask your higher power for what you need. Listen within for an answer. Perhaps you want a friend or loved one to bless you with flowers, touching your head and heart with a single blossom. Maybe there is a song you need to sing. I suggest you keep the ritual short and to the point. A simple prayer or request for help is all that's needed. Large elaborate rites won't work in busy crowded hospital rooms.

JANUARY 22, **Mastery.** *I recognize my personal mastery and honor it in myself and others.*

JANUARY 23, **Release.** *I release the past and make room for more good in my life.*

JANUARY 24, **Love.** *I love myself and surround myself with beauty.*

Buy yourself some fresh flowers today and remind yourself that you are loved in the darkness of winter.

JANUARY 25, **Celebrate.** *I celebrate and utilize my gifts for the good of all.*

Robert Burns, a Scottish poet who was born on this day in 1759, is celebrated with feasts and merriment throughout Scotland.

JANUARY 26, **Warmth.** *In the coldest month of the year I give myself the gift of warmth to myself and share it with others.*

Today is Australia Day, named so because Sydney was founded on this day in 1788. During the northern hemisphere snows, the southern hemisphere is in the middle of summer, therefore January, February, and March are warm and temperate down under. Think for a moment about this. Let yourself imagine what it would be like to be in opposite weather conditions for a change.

JANUARY 27, **Completion.** *Today I notice what I have completed and rest in renewal.*

JANUARY 28, **Letting Go.** *I allow myself to be in the unknown, acknowledging fear and letting it go.*

A Releasing Ceremony

Is there something in your life that you need to let go of? Begin by acknowledging what you are releasing. Then light a candle to help center yourself. Make a drawing of what you are letting go; if it is fear, rage, a thought or an emotion, give it character or shape. Then have a conversation with it. Speak your truth, then take time to listen and hear an answer. Then say good-bye and let yourself grieve if you need to.

If this is a ritual after surgery, any art materials can be used for an image of what you are losing. You can use clay and release the unfired clay figure into a stream. You can use pâpier-maché; paint it and burn it to let go of the spirit of the missing part. Let your intuition and imagination be your guide.

JANUARY 29, **Welcoming.** *I welcome the new and the good into my life.*

JANUARY 30, **Expectancy.** *I postpone doing what is before me, waiting for the good to enter my life.*

JANUARY 31, **Being.** *I release pushing or pulling myself and others along.*

"Do without doing and everything gets done." This ancient Buddhist saying allows you to complete your tasks in full presence, knowing that everything gets done.

Divorce Ritual

Performing a ritual to acknowledge the end of a relationship—whether it be a marriage, a love relationship, or a friendship—can be very healing. The ceremony helps tie up loose ends emotionally and psychically, helping all concerned to move on.

You may find your ex-spouse is not willing to participate with you. It's not necessary to have both partners present. Doing a ritual just for yourself can be very effective, and it may be all you need. Before you start, here are some questions to ask yourself:

1. Do I want to completely sever my relationship with my former spouse?

2. If not, in what ways and for what reasons do I want to remain

connected? If so, are there any other relationships affected by the divorce that I want to maintain (for example, to the spouse's parents, siblings, children, or other relatives)? How will severing this relationship affect those relationships?

3. Is it desirable to perform a ritual of divorce together?

4. If there are children, should we include them? This is not recommended if the children are too young to understand what is happening. On the other hand, children understand symbols more clearly than conceptual language. If they are included, it could also be a way for them to express their feelings about the divorce. I recommend you consult your counselor, minister, rabbi, or therapist for input. Then ask the children if they want to participate, and let them clearly understand what you are doing.

5. What are the aspects of this relationship that I want to divorce?

6. What are the aspects I want to keep?

7. How have I changed as a result of sharing my life with this person—positively and negatively?

8. What new areas of my life can I claim as I look forward to life as a single adult?

9. What am I afraid of?

10. Who would I/we like to include, if anyone, in this rite?

11. What objects would I/we want to include?

12. Where should it take place?

13. How should I/we want to begin it?

14. What will be the focal point of the rite?

15. What is it that I/we need to do to complete this relationship as symbolized in the rite?

16. What do I want to maintain in the relationship?

17. How can I incorporate letting go with the aspects I want to maintain in the relationship into the rite?

18. How will the ritual close?

February

He brought me to the
banqueting house,
and his banner over me
was love.

—Song of Songs 2:4

THE SHORTEST MONTH OF THE YEAR, February's name came from the Latin word *februarius*, meaning to purify. The Romans had a god named Februus, the god of the underworld, and Juno Februis was the mother of Mars, the god of war. Some believe the name came from her because she was the goddess of passionate love. Her rituals of love were celebrated on February 14, which we know today as Saint Valentine's Day. February is called by many other names: The Irish call it *Feabhra;* the Anglo-Saxons called it *Solmonath,* meaning Sun Month, when the sun begins to gradually return after the darkest months; the ancient Franks called it *Horn* or Horning Month for the turning of the year. The full moon in February is called Snow Moon in the backwoods of the United States. The flower of February is primrose, and the birthstone is amethyst.

⌇⌇ Fiddling with February ⌇⌇

According to legend, Romulus, the founder of Rome, described the original Roman calendar with ten months, which did not include

February and January. Then Emperor Numa Pompilius added two months to the calendar, making February the last month of the year and the month of purification by the Romans. Eventually, Julius Caesar revised the calendar and made January instead of March the first month of the year, making February the second month. Caesar also took one day off and added it to the month of July (because it was named after him). Augustus did the same adding an extra day to August, the month named after him, leaving February short two days, except for leap year, when the month has twenty-nine days. So that's why it's the shortest month of the year.

FEBRUARY 1, **Healing.** *I make room for the healing balm of love in my life.*

St. Bridget's Day is celebrated in honor of the ancient goddess known as Bridget, Bride, Brigid, or Brid, the goddess of fire and inspiration. In Ireland, she is the triple goddess of poetry, metalcraft, and healing. In the sixth century, an Irish woman named Bridget, who is said to have been the daughter of a Catholic mother and a Druid father, learned both the faith of the dominant culture, Christianity, and the ancient goddess religion and eventually became an abbess of the Catholic Church. She was a much beloved abbess, who often meditated in the woods near Kildare. The people believed she was the ancient goddess reborn as a healer and spiritual leader of her people. Over the centuries, the two Bridgets have become one with the weaving of folklore and the passing of time.

The festivities for Saint Bridget's Day are feasting and celebrating. The mistress of the house or the servants dress a sheaf of oats in a woman's dress and place it in a basket (called the bride's bed) with a wooden club near it. They cry three times, "Bride is come . . ." before the feast. In other places, the women carry the sheaf around town and prepare a "bride's feast," where men are allowed into the festivities only if they beg at the locked front door.

〰️ St. Bridget's Day Feast 〰️

To celebrate St. Bridget's Day, place a centerpiece on your kitchen table, perhaps a sheaf of wheat in a basket or a flower arrangement, then surround it with candles for the fire of inspiration. You can also add fabric for Bridget's dress and/or symbols of St. Bridget—such as a healing poem, a piece of metal, or some healing herbs—in the basket. Share with your friends or family the significance of the objects and encourage them to add to the arrangement. You can also ask that they share a healing poem or story at dinner or throughout the month when you share meals together. Another idea is to share what inspires each of you in your lives. The answers may surprise you!

FEBRUARY **2**, **Hope.** *I rekindle my heart with a candle flame.*

Today is Candlemas Day. Originally celebrated for the Greek goddess

Demeter who searched for her lost daughter Persephone (who Hades stole) with the light of a candle, Candlemas was appropriated by the Catholic Church by Emperor Justinian to celebrate the day that Mary ritually cleansed herself before bringing her forty-day-old son Jesus to the temple in Jerusalem. Winter being the dark and dreary season that it is, candles help us celebrate the hope that is still aflame in our hearts.

A Candlemas Celebration

Begin with a pot of Earth in the center of a circle. Before you place the candles in the Earth, draw a spiral in the Earth with your finger. (The symbol of the spiral is significant at this time because of the spinning out of the year and the continuation of the growing sun.) Then place the candles in the Earth.

As each person lights her candle, share a poem or story centered on the theme of hope, growth through the darkness, or growth for the infant year. As you finish your sharing, stand if you are not already standing, then clear the space by setting aside the pot of Earth, keeping the candles lit. Join hands and form a circle. Designate a leader and have that person let go with one hand and begin a spiral dance into the center. This is an ancient Celtic dance that celebrates the continuum of life. When the leader gets to the center, he or she turns outward toward his or her open hand. This way the leader is momentarily back to back with the person with whom the other hand is joined. The leader continues dancing between rows of people until he or she chooses to snake around to form the circle again.

When you are finished, come back to the larger circle and hold hands. Send the good energy you have created forward as healing for the coming year. Finish by bringing the pot of Earth with the lit candles back into the center of the circle and blow the candles out in the center together.

FEBRUARY 3, **Lessons.** *I open to the lessons I have learned and surrender to what they are teaching me.*

FEBRUARY 4, **Wholeness.** *I am whole and complete in my being.*

FEBRUARY 5, **Extremes.** *I let the extreme of winter instruct me.*

FEBRUARY 6, **Awareness.** *As I slow down, I deepen my awareness.*

FEBRUARY 7, **Joining Lessons and Wholeness.** *I join with my lessons and expand into more wholeness.*

～～ Chinese New Year ～～

The dates of the Chinese New Year fluctuate from year to year depending on when the second full moon of the year appears. Before the year begins, all accounts, debts, and houses need to be cleaned up. The day is celebrated over a fifteen day period, when gifts, food, and money are exchanged with good wishes for health, happiness, good fortune, and fertility for the new year.

FEBRUARY 8, **Breath.** *Today I allow myself to breath fully, filling my lungs and cleaning my blood with fresh oxygen.*

FEBRUARY 9, **Resistance.** *Honoring my resistance, I give myself space to breathe.*

FEBRUARY 10, **Journey.** *I recognize my journey and honor others on their path.*

FEBRUARY 11, **Power.** *True power lies in the freedom of loving myself and others. I release control of others to their highest good.*

FEBRUARY 12, **Heart.** *I allow my heart to open and close like a flower as needed.*

FEBRUARY 13, **Allowing.** *I allow myself to do and enjoy what I love today.*

FEBRUARY 14, **Love.** *I open to more love today whether that be with myself or other people. I give freely without a thought of return.*

Valentine's Day has often been related to the saint named Valentine; however, the custom of expressing love to your sweetheart on February 14 seems to have more to do with two important ancient customs. One was a medieval belief that birds began mating every February at this time; the other traced back to Roman times, where one drew a lot for love randomly from a box on February 15. The custom was so popular that in the mid-sixteenth century, St. Francis de Sales tried to change the custom for boys to draw the lot of a female saint. The custom of giving cards at this time of year or sending valentines began in the 1800s and has remained popular to this day.

A Lover's Ceremony

The point of this is to find a way to express your love for one another, honoring each other and marking this very important day in some significant way. If you begin with this intention, you are sure to come up with a loving and meaningful rite of relationship. Brainstorm the following ideas together and see what other ideas feel right for you.

Don't discount any ideas. Even if they sound silly, write down what appeals to you. Then go over the list and look at which ideas attract both of you the most. Rituals are like stories and can have a beginning, middle, and end. Tell the story of your intention, excitement, and love together, and you will have your rite of relationship.

1. In a loving way, wash each other's face and hands.
2. Light a candle and pass it around one another in a circle, so you eventually complete a circle of light around the two of you, letting each other know what you love about the other.
3. Light candles of two different colors representing each one of you.
4. Find or create poems that express your love to each other.
5. Tell of your intention to love one another well in the coming year. What do you plan to work on in relationship to one another?

～～ Being with the Beans ～～

February 2 through February 4 marks Setsubun in Japan, or "dividing the seasons," a time for public and private ceremonies, to cast out bad luck and demons and bring in the good. People throw roasted soybeans off the balconies of shrines and throughout their homes while declaring the demons out and the good luck in. This custom was also done in Ancient Rome to feed the spirits of the dead in a ceremony called Lemuria. The word for bean, mame *in Japanese, carries the double meaning of bean and good health.*

FEBRUARY 15, **Flow.** *I go with the flow in my life and allow myself to be directed.*

FEBRUARY 16, **Grace.** *I rest in the abundant good available to me. Every time I experience love, it is grace itself holding me.*

FEBRUARY 17, **Hope.** *I pay attention to the hope that enters my life in the smallest ways, through a reassuring touch, the joy I feel, or someone's kindness.*

FEBRUARY 18, **Challenge.** *I choose to see my challenges as tests of strength and endurance that serve me.*

FEBRUARY 19, **Witness.** *I witness my feeling, my thoughts, and my actions as I move through my day.*

FEBRUARY 20, **Transition.** *I take especially good care of myself when I am facing a transition because of the extra stress I am experiencing.*

〰〰 Remedy for Those Winter Blues 〰〰

When you've got the winter blues, try Bach Flower Remedies available at your local health food store. These remedies help ease emotional stress and tension: for gloom try mustard or rose, for fretfulness try chicory, for discouragement try gentian, for general emotional stress try "rescue remedy."

FEBRUARY 21, **Words.** *All my words are important. Today I will pay special attention to the words that I use.*

Today is the day that the Romans celebrated their version of the Day of the Dead, celebrated by the Mexican people in October. On Feralia (from the Latin *ferre* or to ferry or carry), the Romans left bits of grain, beans, flowers, and bread-soaked wine, to help the ghosts ferry across the River Styx.

FEBRUARY 22, **Divine Order.** *My life is filled with divine order, and all my relatives, friends, and loved ones are in harmony with divine order. I release them to their highest good and retain unconditional love.*

The day after the Romans honored the dead, they honored the living, those who remained behind, in Caristia, from the word *cara*, meaning dear. On this day, all feuds and challenges were set aside to creates feast and celebration of the love remaining among remaining family members. The peace goddess Concordia ruled this day with cornucopia and olive branches as her symbols.

Honoring Parents

Today, if your parents are living, take a moment to honor them. Too often people wait to honor their parents at their funeral, instead of expressing love to them while they are still alive. Showing them your appreciation, however, can be very healing and create deep levels of communication.

Even though many people need to heal their past with their mothers and fathers, there comes a point when there needs to be an end to the process. Once you figure out what needs can be met by your family of origin and what needs can't, it is easier to let go of the expectation that they should meet your needs. Then you are free to find ways to give yourself what you missed.

It's helpful to the process of reconciliation to realize what you did receive as a child and appreciate your family for those gifts.

1. Start by writing down the things you learned as a child, say a random number of five, ten, or twenty things. This will help you flush out what you may have forgotten. What you learned from your parents could be as simple as tying one's shoe, learning to cook or play baseball, or receiving your first doll.

2. Next make a list of things you needed as a child that you didn't get. This is your childhood wish list. Today, as an adult, give yourself those things or ask a friend to help you. For closure, it's important that you get the things that you didn't receive and that you clear up any resentments that may still be lingering. You may want to give each thing to yourself in a ritual way, drawing a circle of love around you and letting yourself cry.

3. Find something from your past or create something that you value and set a time aside to create a rite around it with your parents. Perhaps inviting them out to dinner or giving it to them at Thanksgiving can make it a unique and special celebration.

Appreciating your parents is not always easy. Some people have experienced abusive upbringings and appreciating their parents is not possible. Others are confronted with fears of rejection or abandonment, which are intensified because of the wounds they may have received as children. It may feel as though you are putting your head in the tiger's mouth to express sincere feelings to your family.

Healing your fear can be a good reason for you to do this rite. If you keep in mind that showing your appreciation and healing your fears are your intention, you can release the outcome and create an atmosphere of safety for you and your parents. Remember, if you approach your family with sincerity, there won't be room for them to make light of an authentic gesture.

FEBRUARY 23, **Boundaries**. *I set my boundaries for my highest good with ease.*

FEBRUARY 24, **Mourning**. *I allow myself to grieve the losses I have suffered. I am at peace.*

In order to find the inner strength to move forward in our lives, we need to answer these questions: How can we reconcile losses that may make us feel like a victim? And how can we deal with the loss as part of the flow of our life?

Bringing Light out of Darkness

First we need to see loss as a natural part of living. Mourning helps us let go, and it gives way to new life. Remember, however, grieving doesn't happen all at once but in waves that rise and fall like an ocean tide.

Secondly, we need to know that anything bad that happens has a lesson in it. The lesson of loss is to learn to let go.

Finally, we must notice the victim or martyr energy in us. Somehow that energy manifests itself because we are not feeling loved or accepted by ourselves or others. It is up to us to recognize our victim pattern and to love that pattern into wholeness through loving attention. Imagine that part of yourself as a personality with characteristics that are distinct. Name the victim; it could even be a funny name, like "Marvelous Marytr." Then imagine that this character is carrying on a discussion with the part of yourself that wants to be more healthy and happy, or with your higher power. Be firm and loving with this part of you. Sometimes you have to practice tough love with yourself. Keep sending the Marvelous Marytr love and watch the changes. If we truly want to live in more harmony, love, respect, and safety, we need to see how the martyr in us may affect our relationship with ourself and with others. Really grieving our losses and letting them go helps us to give up martyrdom.

FEBRUARY 25, **Control.** *I release control over everything but my affairs. I recognize that the only things I can control in my life are my thoughts.*

FEBRUARY 26, **Criticism.** *I watch my inner critic with awareness. I forgive my inner critic for its judgment of me and others.*

FEBRUARY **27**, **Decisions.** *I make decisions easily and smoothly. If I come to an impasse, I turn it over to my higher power and allow the right decision to come to me.*

〜〜 Honoring Death 〜〜

February seems to be a time when people pass on, especially in cold climates. Here are suggestions for a funeral, which could be created for a person you have lost or for something that has ended in your life.

    1. *How is the deceased represented?*

    2. *Will he or she be buried, cremated? Will there be flowers, candles, and so on in his or her honor?*

    3. *Where do you want to hold the service?*

    4. *Who would you want to officiate?*

    5. *Is there someone who can handle the details such as newspaper announcements, flowers, memorial donations, and so on?*

    6. *Who else wants or needs to be involved?*

    7. *What songs, poems, and stories are there to share?*

FEBRUARY **28**, **Nourishment.** *I nourish my body with food that is healthy for me.*

Nourishment in the winter seems especially comforting. Why not try this wonderfully warming soup tonight?

Mid-Winter Pumpkin Soup

1 medium-sized pumpkin
2 cups water
½ cup soy milk or regular milk (chocolate milk if preferred)
½ cup butter or margarine
1–2 large onions, minced
3–4 sticks celery, chopped
2–3 leeks, chopped
2 teaspoons nutmeg
1 teaspoon turmeric
1 teaspoon each chervil and/or marjoram
1 ½ teaspoon basil
4–6 bouillon cubes, vegetable or chicken
Salt and pepper to taste

Slice a medium pumpkin in half scraping the seeds out, then turn it upside down in a baking pan with 1½ cups water. Bake at 350 degrees for forty to sixty minutes. Use a toothpick or fork through the skin to test if it is done. (Or cut the pumpkin into sections and boil it in water for thirty to forty minutes until tender. Peel the skin off the flesh and reserve water for the soup base.) You can do this ahead and freeze the pumpkin to use later.

Scrape the insides of the pumpkin into a mixing bowl. For 2 cups of pumpkin, mix in a ½ cup milk or soy milk (chocolate milk or chocolate/carob soy milk adds a special flavor). Blend thoroughly with milk. Set aside.

In a frying pan, melt butter or margarine and sauté onions, celery, leeks, nutmeg, turmeric, chervil and/or marjoram, and basil until tender.

In a large soup kettle, dissolve bouillon cubes in remaining ¼ cup of water. Add the pumpkin and onion mixture, then salt and pepper to taste (white pepper if you have it). Be sure to stir in love with every step. The mixture should be thick and hearty. Bring to a boil and simmer on low heat for at least twenty minutes. Serves 6.

FEBRUARY **29**, **Order**. *My life evolves naturally from the order in the Universe and the order I bring to my life.*

Leap year occurs every four years, when the Gregorian calendar compensates for the natural order of the Earth. She takes 365 days, five hours, and forty-eight minutes to revolve around the sun, not just 365 days. And so by the fourth year, we are really out of sync, and an additional day, February 29, is add to compensate for the difference. It is also the time (by law in Scotland since 1288) when it is proper for a woman to ask a man for his hand in marriage.

March

From dust I rise,
And out of nothing now awake...;

—from *The Salutation* by
Thomas Traherne

THE ROMAN GOD OF WAR IS MARS, born on March 1. The way the Romans celebrated his birth was to pay respect to his mother Juno, the patron goddess of childbirth. Women walked miles to pay homage to Juno, who conceived Mars while touching a wildflower. Originally the first month of the year, March was made the third month by Julius Caesar. The Irish call March *Mi an Mharta*. The Anglo-Saxons called it *Hrethmonath*, commemorating Hera's Month, who is the Greek equivalent of the Roman Juno, and the Franks called it *Lentzinmanoth*, or Renewal Month. In the southeastern backwoods, the full moon in March is known as the Worm Moon or Sap Moon because it is the month when the sap begins to rise; the eastern Native American tribes (and many Vermonters) collect sap from maple trees for sugaring. The birthstones for March are the bloodstone and aquamarine. The flower is the violet.

MARCH 1, **Birth.** *I give birth to the light in me. I rest and feel ease in the heart of my being. A light glows there, safe inside me.*

MARCH 2, **Change.** *Wind is blowing change into my life; I am growing; I love myself unconditionally without reservation.*

MARCH 3, **Teachers.** *I look to the people at work as my allies; those who challenge me are my teachers. All is well.*

MARCH 4, **Bounty.** *Spirit is the source of my supply. I ask for support from the bounty of the Universe.*

~~~ A Winter Feast ~~~

If you have the February blues, add to a good meal the treat of cloth napkins and rings, candles, and candle holders, and you have a feast. Even eating a simple meal like soup and salad takes on elegance and beauty when eaten at a beautiful table setting.

MARCH 5, **Waking Up.** *Today as the weather changes outside, I know I am waking up to more of myself inside. Even though it is uncomfortable some of the time, I can feel gratitude welling up in me.*

March 5 is Isis Day, as celebrated by the ancient Egyptians. Isis is equivalent to Juno, goddess of feminine fertility. She is the goddess who refused to accept her husband's brutal dismemberment by Set, their brother and god of the desert, and she was the inventor of the sail. With the help of the other gods and goddesses, Isis reconstructed her husband Osiris, who overcame death with Isis' help. Afterward, she gave birth to Horus, who became pharaoh of Egypt, and Osiris, who became god of the underworld.

In Corinth, Isis remains the sailor's patron goddess of water. Every year at this time, the Romans hold a festival with garlands, lamps, torches, and merriment, with a parade of sorts making its way to the sea, carrying an unmanned, carved boat as a gift to the goddess of the sea, the stars, and the lovers of the Universe.

MARCH 6, **Gratitude.** *Thankfulness is like a spring gushing out of the Earth: fresh, renewing, life giving. I walk today with a grateful heart.*

〜〜 Isis Day 〜〜

Try these suggestions to celebrate the sea, the stars, and the God and Goddess within. At your dinner table or on your altar, float a garland of flowers in honor of the gifts that Isis brought, namely sailing, fishing, and the renewal of life through water. You may want to place a candle to burn in the center. You can also use the soothing essential oils of rose water or lavender in the bath tonight while you give thanks for water as the deliverer of life.

MARCH 7, **Pleasure.** *I give pleasure to my body today, as I renew my love of myself. I take the time for self-massage, enjoying the texture of my skin. I notice where I feel sensation and where I do not. I send love to those places that cannot feel.*

～～ Self-Massage ～～

Take some time before you go to sleep to massage yourself. Begin by taking three deep breaths to center yourself. Start with your feet and use a lotion or oil. Rub gently or firmly between the bones and work your way up to your ankles and calves. When your get to your thighs, pay attention to the outside and inside. There are acupressure points that may be sore and could use some gentle pressure. Rub in a circular direction or hold the sore points until they gently release. As you rub, notice when they are releasing, restoring you to more ease and relaxation. Continue with your abdomen, massaging from right to left in a circle around your belly button, following the movement of your large intestine. Continue with your arms and neck and shoulders, pausing at spots that need particular attention.

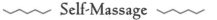

MARCH 8, **Respect.** *Today I witness respect from others, as I respect myself. I honor others for who they are, and I acknowledge them.*

March 8 is International Woman's Day, the one day of the year when, besides the men whose birthdays are celebrated as national holidays, women are celebrated. Originally inspired by a Ladies Garment Workers' strike in the 1850s and celebrated in Russia before it came to the United States, it is now a time for both women and men to honor the work that women do supporting the home, family, and global economy.

MARCH 9, **Acceptance.** *What is it in me that cannot be acknowledged? Do I see this quality in others around me?*

Take one difficult thing about yourself and sit with it for a moment, in the car, while you meditate, when you are about to doze off to sleep. Walk with it instead of fighting it, then watch what happens!

MARCH 10, **Thoughts.** *I am in charge of my thoughts; I can be with them, cancel them, support positive thoughts that enhance my life. All is well.*

MARCH 11, **Love Heals All Things.** *Today, I will not try to fix, manipulate, or cajole my fears. I will just be with them and send them love.*

MARCH 12, **Authority.** *I have authority over my life and affairs. My decisions form my path; the lessons I need to learn form my path. All else is unfolding according to a larger plan of which I am an integral part.*

MARCH 13, **Letting Go.** *I can begin release control by breathing ease into my body, mind, spirit, and emotions. I let myself cry or laugh, feel angry or sad, and I turn my cares and concerns over to the Universal Source of Love.*

MARCH 14, **Guidance.** *My guide, angel, helper is at work for me, and I acknowledge this. Calling on the highest and wisest source of guidance, I listen without judgment and open with faith to the messages.*

~~~ **Five-Minute Balancing Meditation** ~~~

What is trying to be born in you today? Take a couple of deep breaths and focus on your heart center. Imagine there is a garden in your heart. Invite your feminine and masculine energies to enter one at a time. Let them interact. How are they together? Are they balanced, in harmony, at odds, larger or smaller than each other? If there is conflict between them, have them discuss it. Invite your higher self in to resolve their disharmony. If they are not in conflict, let them greet each other and embrace, however you wish. What is it they wish to give birth to together in you? How can they assist you in your work or daily life? Ask them and listen.

MARCH 15, **Creation**. *Today I allow my creativity to flow, creating new life changes.*

In Japan, March 15 marks the day to celebrate the Togata Henen-Sai Phallus Festival. This festival celebrates the birth of the Japanese islands in a wild mating spree between Izanami and Izanagi, Japan's goddess and god of the earth and sky. Their lovemaking also created a host of other deities, including the fire god, Ho-Masubi. When, in the course of their spatting and lovemaking, Izanami could take no more and she lay dying, her excrement produced more deities. As Izanai mourned her death, according to *The World Holiday Book*, "His right eye secreted the sun goddess, his left the moon god, and from his nose oozed the guardian of the sea, Susanoo."

MARCH 16, **Wholeness.** *I am complete and whole in myself. I call those parts that are not feeling their wholeness to me and join with them in love.*

～～ Money Meditation ～～

Feeling short of funds? Try this one-minute meditation as often as you wish during the day. Sit in a comfortable chair, or stand up, feet shoulder-width apart. Affirm to yourself, "The Great Spirit is the source of my supply. There is abundance all around me." Then visualize yourself with greenbacks floating through your energy field. Let them fall like rain. You can also affirm, "I am taken care of by God. I am nurtured and loved, and all my needs are met." Repeat as often as you wish. Don't forget to be grateful and thanks for what you already have.

MARCH 17, **Abundance.** *Money is energy, and it demonstrates my commitment to life. When I share my resources, I show my love and commitment to myself, to those I love, and to the Earth.*

St. Patrick's Day is celebrated on March 17. Green colors everything from the Chicago River to beer and hair at local pubs. The feeling is celebratory and abundant, and it coincides with the end of winter and the advent of spring. When you are generous, you feel abundant. What can you do today to celebrate what is abundant in your life?

MARCH 18, **Heart.** *I center myself today in my heart, feeling love radiate from my center.*

If you feel threatened or challenged today, simply return to your heart, take a deep breath, and center yourself there.

MARCH 19, **Responsibility.** *I choose to be responsible for my life. There is nothing I cannot handle if I know when to ask for help. I walk in balance in my life and affairs.*

5

Spring:
Season of Promise

Help us to be the always hopeful gardeners of the spirit who know that without darkness nothing comes to birth as without light nothing flowers.

—May Sarton

DIRECTION: South, Earth

ASTROLOGICAL SIGNS:

Aries: March 21–April 19   *Taurus:* April 20–May 20
Gemini: May 21–June 20

MARCH 21 MARKS THE SPRING (vernal) equinox. The first day of spring has traditionally been a time to celebrate the advent of longer days and shorter nights. On the Mayan calendar, it is the beginning of the year, according to Hunbatz Man, an international spokesman for the Mayan people. The Mayans are the only civilization who are known to have two calendars, one based on the solar system like the Gregorian Calendar, which has 365 days. The second one is a sacred calendar with 260 days called *Tzolkin*, which revolves according to various sacred numbers that have to do with crops and the changes of the year honoring various gods and goddesses.

The ancient Mayans were very advanced in astronomy and numerology. It is from their calendar that the Harmonic Convergence was made popular in 1987. It corresponded to the end of a 400-year cycle and the advent of the coming new age. The old Mayan calendar officially ended in 1995. In 1997, the Mayan people are introducing a new calendar for the coming cycle called *Pun Benkik;* their new calendar corresponding to the 365-day calendar is called *Haab.*

In the Norse tradition, spring days get longer with the return of the goddess Iduna, who bears the magic apples of life, bringing more light to the world. The days become brighter and the sun warmer and stronger after the vernal equinox.

Because spring weather is unstable and is generally a time of growth, chills, and thaws, spring's primary symbol is the equidistant cross. This stands in Christianity for the crucifixion, but it predates the advent of Christianity and was used to symbolize relationships. According to Angeles Arrien's *Signs of Life*, "The equidistant cross, the plus sign, universally symbolizes the process of relationship and integration. This is a coupling, synthesizing, integrating and balancing process. . . . It is a symbol that demonstrates integration and balanced connection."

This symbol is significant for spring because while the Earth, the weather, and the season are seeking balance, it is not always achieved. When we seek balance, we are not in balance. Like all changes, however, the seeking is part of the process—the seeking is half of the fun.

⌇⌇ Symbols and Key Words for Spring ⌇⌇

Relations, roots, grounding, Earth, healing, home, stability, soil, inheritance, the color red, metal, stones, equidistant cross symbolizing relationships, the planting of crops. A bowl of Earth, or a red cloth can be used to honor this direction in rituals.

MARCH 20, **Commitment.** *I review my commitments, and I honor those commitments that I want to keep, and allow for change with the commitments I want to transform.*

∼∼ An Earthy Spring Facial ∼∼

Whether you are a man or a woman, there is nothing like a facial to feel renewed. Get yourself some facial mud from your local health food store. Wash your face thoroughly with warm water, using a warm washcloth to open pores. Smooth on the mud and let it dry. Rinse and splash your face with cool water. If you can get a larger supply, and you have a partner, you can do each other's backs or bodies. Shower off together.

MARCH 21, **Self-Care.** *I allow self-care a priority in my healing and rejuvenation.*

MARCH 22, **Communication.** *I pay close attention to communication today, understanding that I am responsible for my words and actions.*

MARCH 23, **Freedom.** *My soul is a free agent; it does what is best for my relationship to the Divine; it allows me to choose and re-choose every day.*

MARCH 24, **Waiting.** *Like the planting of crops, I accomplish a great deal while I wait for life to blossom.*

A Baby Ritual

Spring is the time of new beginnings, so what better time to celebrate an impending birth? If you are welcoming a baby into the world, what are the most important feelings you have to express to your spouse, to the arriving child, and to the rest of your supportive circle?

You may want to incorporate necessary projects, such as painting the baby's room or buying furniture, into the rite. Are there elements representing growth and new life that have meaning for you? Some couples have planted sweet peas in a pot or a tree to commemorate their child's arrival.

Inviting friends or family can also help you transition into your new role as parents. Do they have stories of their own that would be helpful? Maybe your parents will tell the story of your birth.

～～ Greeting the New Day ～～

In many cultures, the tradition of greeting the sun, watching Mother Earth and Father Sky lovingly part one another, is part of spiritual practice. Here is a way to create a morning greeting to each newborn day, which Sue Patton Thoele suggests in her book The Woman's Book of Spirit: *Close your eyes and imagine yourself waking. How do you normally feel? Are you happy with the way you greet the day? If the answer is no, imagine how you would like to change your greeting. Are you smiling? What do you say? Slowly, gently visualize yourself, in the perfect, right time and way, awaken to the gift of a pure, new day. Greet it in the fresh way that you imagined. How does that feel?*

Sometimes in a ritual of welcoming, there may be some grief as well. This is a momentous time, and life changes a lot when children are born. It is important to honor all of your feelings. People often need to grieve the past before they can take hold of the future.

MARCH 25, **Choice.** *I make sound choices for myself and those I love.*

MARCH 26, **Holding.** *I release whatever it is that I am holding onto, unless I need the lessons of holding. Holding on to those things that I care about, I release them to their highest good.*

MARCH 27, **Containment.** *I accept containment to gather my power.*

MARCH 28, **Release.** *I heal and release the past and open to a brighter future.*

MARCH 29, **Challenge.** *I accept the challenges set before me, knowing nothing is beyond my capabilities, if I allow myself to grow.*

〰️ Purim 〰️

Purim (March 12 in 1998; March 2 in 1999; March 21 in 2000) is celebrated during the full moon in March or April. This Jewish religious holiday celebrates the time when Esther saved the Jews from being massacred by Haman, a prime minister of the Persian king Ahasuerus. Haman himself was hung for his treachery. Purim is the plural of pur, *which means* lot or chance *in Hebrew.*

MARCH **29**, **Sprouting.** *I watch the sprouts in the Earth emerge as a sign of encouragement for my growth in my work and my relationships.*

MARCH **31**, **Blossoming.** *I nurture the blossoms in my life.*

〰 Planting Good Wishes 〰

Take some paper white narcissus, tulips, daffodils, or other spring bulbs and nestle them into some rocks in a bowl of water. Plant each bulb with the intention you began your year with, or set some new intentions for the spring. This is a great thing to do with kids, especially little ones in school.

April

One joy dispels a hundred cares.

—Chinese proverb

THE FOURTH MONTH OF THE YEAR was named after the Greek goddess Aphrodite. The Anglo-Saxons named the month *Eastermonath* after the goddess Eoste, which is where the word *Easter* comes from. The Irish call this month *Aibrean*. Also known as the month of the Pink Moon, it is the time of the Earth opening to seeds and the budding of new growth. The flowers of April are the sweat pea and daisy, and the birthstone is the diamond. April is also the time of the trickster, the fool, and the god Loki, from northern European traditions, which is why April 1 is still commemorated as April Fool's Day.

Since the weather fluctuates in most areas of the northern hemisphere quite a lot in April, with warm thaws and sudden freezes, it is a time of tricky weather. Not unlike the beginning of love, when one is uncertain of a new partner's mood swings, changes, and possibilities.

APRIL 1, **Humor.** *Today I celebrate the wisdom of the fool or the trickster. I risk bringing humor to all the situations of my life, so long as I do not cause harm, embarrassment, or ill will in the process. I recognize that reversing my flow of energy brings to me a new flow of possibilities.*

APRIL 2, **Fluidity.** *I flow with love into the areas that need love in my life.*

APRIL 3, **Receptive.** *I am receptive to new and surprising changes that are coming with spring.*

APRIL 4, **Sufficient.** *What I have is sufficient, and I am grateful for it.*

APRIL 5, **Conception.** *This is the time of planting and conceiving new ideas, new directions, new realities.*

APRIL 6, **Seamless.** *I notice the ease with which my life can flow at times. Today I consciously align myself with this energy.*

APRIL 7, **Bright.** *I welcome the brightness of the sun as radiance within me grows.*

〜〜 Passover and Easter 〜〜

Passover and Easter are tied closely together. Both holidays are about deliverance from human suffering and have significance during this time of the year, with the deliverance from winter of the spring weather. The Christian holiday commemorates the death and resurrection of Jesus and the renewal of faith, while the seven-day Jewish holiday commemorates the Jewish flight from Egypt and the Jewish escape from persecution by the grace of God. Matzo, an unleavened bread, taken out of the ovens before it had risen in the rush to escape from the Egyptians, and other foods are eaten in commemoration of this event.

The Easter traditions of the Easter Bunny hiding the eggs are taken from ancient pagan festivals of fertility. The rabbit is a common symbol of fertility and purity, the egg an obvious one, while the children discovering the eggs represents birth. The deeper significance of the cosmic egg reflecting the human energy field should also not be lost in celebration of this significant time of planting and renewal.

APRIL 8, **Fulfilling**. *I am fulfilling my destiny with joy and love for myself and others.*

APRIL 9, **Grounding**. *I pay attention to the Earth today, as well as my connection to it. I am aware that I am supported with every step.*

APRIL 10, **Balance**. *I walk in balance in my life and know that I find balance by sometimes being out of balance.*

APRIL 11, **Fun**. *I play and allow myself to enjoy life.*

APRIL 12, **Laughter**. *As the best medicine, I enjoy a good laugh to clear any thoughts of depression or gloom.*

APRIL 13, **Anger**. *I recognize my anger and allow it to find expression in healthy ways.*

APRIL 14, **Smiles**. *I brighten my day with a bouquet of smiles.*

Welcoming Home

This ritual can be used for several occasions: naming a newborn, blessing a baby (whether she or he has just been born or is an adopted older child), or welcoming home someone who has been away for a long time. Young children can enjoy blessing others with water, as well as receiving the blessing themselves.

A rose, a candle, and water are simple, meaningful tools for blessing your new arrival. The rose signifies love, budding, blossoming, beauty, and peace. Water represents cleansing, emotion, and flow and is synonymous with the west. Besides bringing a focal point to the rite, the candle represents the light of the soul, higher intention, unity, love, and harmony. The yellow of the flame also represents the east, a new beginning.

Take the rose and float it in water. Light a candle and place it on the table nearby. Stir the water and tell the child or person what your good wishes are for them, then sprinkle a little water onto their heads, hands, hearts, or all three places. Pass the bowl from person to person until you complete the circle. Close by blowing the candle out all together.

APRIL 15, **Vision.** *My vision is clear and full of new awareness as I move into spring.*

APRIL 16, **Listening.** *Today I take the time to really listen to my family, friends, and coworkers.*

APRIL 17, **Flavor.** *Today I pay attention to the flavor of foods and the amazing variety that I experience.*

APRIL 18, **Air.** *I pause to notice three breaths.*

Today, take some time to ask yourself: What are the scents I gather from the air? How does air expand my awareness? How clean is the air that I breathe every day? These molecules are the same ones that have circulated the Earth for eons. They are the same ones Buddha and Christ inhaled.

APRIL 19, **Rain.** *I am cleansed by the rains that feed the Earth with nutrients and new life.*

~~~ Spring Tonic ~~~

Try a Bach Flower remedy of crab apple for a spring cleanser. Taken as directed, the essence supports an energetic spring cleaning.

APRIL 20, **Cleansing.** *The cleansing of rain makes way for new growth and life to emerge.*

APRIL 21, **Failures into Flowers.** *Today, I bless my failures and turn them into lessons learned.*

When you reflect on the past, do you notice that your places of real growth are the lessons you've learned through failure? Take a moment and reflect on three failures in your life. Now list what you learned from them and congratulate yourself!

APRIL 22, **Earth.** *I celebrate Earth Day and support clean air and water to nurture my home, family, and community.*

Earth Day

Earth Day has been widely celebrated in the United States since 1970. Invented by environmentalists to draw attention to the peril we humans have put the Earth in, it has now been adopted by communities across the United States to help in cleaning lakes and rivers, and highways and road-ways—to celebrate through Earth-healing rituals, bike-a-thons, and Earth-day runs.

The most critical areas concerning the planet regard clean air and clean water. Blessing the water that comes into your home and praying for it to be clean are ways you can help. Another way is to keep up on leg-islation that affects our air and water quality. There are socially responsi-ble companies that can help. Working Assets Long Distance service, for example, provides to its customers a list of congressional decisions that affect everyone and gives customers an opportunity to donate money every month to those nonprofit organizations that are supporting clean air, clean water, and a host of other services. Their rates are competitive. To find out more, call 1-800-548-2567.

〜〜 An April Shower 〜〜

Today, begin your shower giving thanks to the water, giving thanks to the air that you breathe, and standing in the shower, imagine that it is blessing you. Imagine one or two things that you want to release, set your intention, and let the water carry it away. Continue the release process as you dry yourself off.

APRIL 23, **Enlightenment.** *Spring cleaning of my home, body, mind, and heart help me to lighten up. Today I become lighter, by releasing the trials and challenges, remembering the lessons but forgiving the hurts. All is well.*

APRIL 24, **Virtue.** *I celebrate the goodness that is all around me, within myself, and in the faces of those I meet.*

APRIL 25, **Doubt.** *Like a rain cloud, doubts cloud my horizon and bring me more into myself and the moment.*

APRIL 26, **Understanding.** *I foster understanding and love between people through good communication and right action.*

APRIL 27, **Conflict.** *Conflict helps me see where I am growing, where I need to expand my view, and where I can give love to a power struggle that has no love in it.*

APRIL 28, **Work.** *I enjoy the pressure of work, which helps me to grow when I must meet the challenges presented.*

APRIL 29, **Empty.** *I empty myself like a glass of water, so that I can refill my life with renewed energy and vitality.*

APRIL 30, **Rest.** *Giving myself the rest I need, I can face the new day knowing I am restored and renewed.*

May

Speak to the Earth,
and it shall teach thee.

—Job 12:8

THIS MONTH'S NAME COMES ORIGINALLY from the Greek god Maia, who is the leader of the Pleiades, or seven sisters, and the mother of Hermes, the messenger god. May is truly the month of spring, the first month of full blossoming and growth. The Irish call this month *Medb* (Maeve) and the fairy queen Mab in Shakespeare derives her name from Maia.

The Irish also call this *Cedsoman* or *Ceadamh*, meaning the first summer, and May 1 is the holy day Betaine (*taine* meaning "fire"). May was also known as "thrice milk month" or *Thrimilcmonath* because cows give three times a day during May. The Franks called this month Joy Month or *Winnemanoth*.

~~~ Sacred Sex ~~~

For your May Day ritual, have you and your partner massage each
other before you make love. Use a rose or musk scented oil. When you
connect, imagine a ring of light moving up your spine (if you are a
woman), down your lover's back and through his genitals into you.
If you are two women or two men, imagine the connection coming

from one of you and moving through the other. This way you give and receive in a cycle. It also helps to sustain orgasm.

MAY 1, **Joy.** *I encourage joy today in my life and in my world. I celebrate this first day of May with gratitude and joy.*

May Day

This is one of the major Celtic festivals of the year, signifying the mystic union between the male and female principles. Since the time of the Romans, everyone in the village slept out of doors in the woods on May Eve, a tradition that culminated in lovemaking as a grand celebration of life. When sex outside marriage was declared a sin by the Church, this tradition was discouraged by the clergy throughout Europe.

Today people celebrate the fertility of spring on this day with a May Pole dance, weaving bright, colorful ribbons in and out of a central pole (a phallic symbol) with other celebrants. On the ribbons are written their intentions for the flowering of spring. Another tradition is for couples to jump over a pot of fire and declare what it is they want in their life.

MAY 2, **Rejuvenation.** *I give my body massage or exercise to rejuvenate my spirit.*

MAY 3, **Warmth.** *The warmth of the spring rains nourishes me as well as the Earth.*

MAY 4, **Bright.** *When the sun is out, it brightens my day. I pay attention to what supports my bright spirit.*

∿∿ Fabulous Foot Massage ∿∿

Combine eight ounces of almond oil with ten to twenty drops of tea tree oil and a few drops of oil of lavender, sandalwood, rose, or chamomile. Mix well. Apply to your feet or ask someone else to do it for you.

MAY 5, **Dawning.** *Like the lengthening days, I am dawning to new awareness of my path and pleasures.*

MAY 6, **Improvement.** *Always there is need in my life and home for improvement. I choose one thing to accomplish.*

MAY 7, **Loss.** *With every loss, I acknowledge that the pruning of my soul takes place. There is new growth under the tears that need to be shed.*

MAY 8, **Kindness.** *I watch the world change as I demonstrate kindness to others.*

MAY 9, **Good News.** *Today I look for the good news that brightens my day.*

MAY 10, **Nutrition.** *I am willing to eat well today, taking foods that support my health and well-being.*

MAY 11, **Truth.** *I tell the truth today with kindness without exception, and let the consequences fall where they may.*

MAY 12, **Pay Attention.** *I pay attention to what has truth and meaning.*

~~~ Mother's Day ~~~

A day commemorating mothers everywhere, this holiday is accompanied by gifts and flowers for Mother. It began in England as Mothering Sunday, during mid-Lent before Easter. In the United States, Julie Ward Howe first suggested it in 1872. Several other people started celebrations and observances, until Anna Jarvis of Grafton, West Virginia, started a national campaign. She began the custom of wearing a colored carnation to church on the second Sunday in May if your mother was living and a white one if she had passed away. Through her church, Andrews Methodist Episcopal, a representative brought a resolution to the church convention in Minneapolis in 1912, recognizing Anna Jarvis as the founder of Mother's Day. Two years later, President Woodrow Wilson signed a joint resolution of congress recommending that the nation observe Mother's Day.

MAY 13, **Mother.** *I trust my ability to mother myself, whether I have received good mothering from others or not.*

MAY **14, Limitations.** *My limitations show where I need to grow. As I come up against my limitations, I honor them as a way of showing me where I need to release.*

Carabao Festival, Philippines

May 14 honors the patron saint of field workers, Saint Isidore. Born in 1070, outside of Madrid, he spent his life working the fields and performing miracles. In the Philippines, Isidore is patron of the water buffalo, or carabao, which ploughs the fields. Farmers decorate their water buffalo with garlands, hitch them to flower carts, and take them to local villages where the priests bless them. Afterward, the animals are raced across fields in contests, and villagers gather to feast and celebrate the planting of the fields.

MAY **15, Acceptance.** *As I grow in love of myself, I accept myself on every level. I notice that I more easily accept others as part of the process.*

〰 Expect a Miracle 〰

Miracles come to us every day, although sometimes we don't recognize them. A kind word, a loving gesture, a simple loving thought— imagine for a moment a miracle that you would appreciate in your life, then give yourself the pleasure of having it handed to you. Now surround this thought in a pink bubble of love and release it like a prayer request. Do not pull the bubble back to you, just let it go like a helium-filled balloon. Then open yourself to receiving what you asked for in a surprising way.

MAY 16, **Warmth.** *As the sun warms the Earth in spring and flowers begin to appear, I am warm in the knowledge that I am in harmony with the Earth and the seasons.*

MAY 17, **Barriers.** *I notice the barriers that limit me; I rest with them, as though I am resting against a door that will open when the time is appropriate.*

MAY 18, **Patience.** *Today I remember that there is no rushing the natural process of life unfolding. I wait patiently for what I want to open and blossom.*

MAY 19, **Resolve.** *I Resolve myself to the flow of life, and accept the good that comes my way.*

MAY 20, **Goal.** *My goals set the tone for the process of life that I am in. While I can accomplish my goals, I relax into the process of change that my goals set for me.*

House Blessing

Since this is a time of cleaning and rebirth, here are some suggestions for making your home a more sacred environment:

1. Ask yourself, your family, or housemates: What do I want my home to be? or, How do I want it to feel? To facilitate this, you can create a playful kitchen table discussion that will help bring the members of your home together. Make a list of agreed upon qualities. If there are

children, encourage them to write out and/or decorate their intention with crayons, pens, or craft supplies.

2. When you have your combined list of desired qualities, you can create a simple rite of dedication by lighting a candle and nailing the list upon the wall, officially proclaiming it to be a touchstone for your home. This motto should not become law, but a guideline. If you or someone else need it to change, it's time to rededicate!

3. Be sure to allow everyone to contribute to the rite as well as to the list of qualities. This is important in order for each person to feel part of what you are jointly creating.

MAY 21, **Sparks.** *I allow the sparks of inspiration to flow through me. I feel life and energy awaken in me.*

MAY 22, **Opening.** *I watch the opening of flowers and trees around me. I trust the flow of opening and closing in my heart.*

~~~ Soul Garden ~~~

May is the time to reconnect with the Earth after a long winter, and there is nothing like a garden to create that connection. A garden can also be a sanctuary from everyday stress, while the beauty that you create is an art form. Of course you can appreciate someone else's efforts, too, or the city park. Here's a meditation inspired by Sue Patton Thoele's The Woman's Book of Spirit: *Take a moment and reflect on the garden of your soul. Your soul needs may be different than an actual garden's needs, but the process of planting is the same.*

*Spend some time with your heart, and see what it needs. Then, like
a gardener, cultivate and nurture your heart's garden to make blossoming possible.*

MAY 23, **Rest.** *I notice that nature is not always constant at any stage, but constantly moving through cycles of life. I awaken to the rhythms of the Universe
and the cycles that inspire me.*

MAY 24, **Holding.** *I notice what I am holding onto. I stay with it and allow
myself to feel my grip.*

MAY 25, **Fire.** *Through the fire of transformation, I make way with the new in
my life in perfect order in the Universe.*

MAY 26, **Fullness.** *Opening to the fullness of choices, I am empowered to feast
on my life.*

MAY 27, **Leisure.** *Allowing myself the downtime that I need to spring forth into
creativity, I see leisure as a necessary time to rest before the rising spring of
inspiration comes.*

MAY 28, **Graduation.** *At this time of graduations, I honor the work I have done
to accomplish my tasks. I open to my future with energy and excitement. I
enjoy the celebration marking my transition from one phase of life to the other.*

Life is full of many endings and new beginnings. One of the most common is moving; the average American moves every four years.

Moving Ritual

Whether you are married or single, moving your home can be life-altering. Even if you move within the same town, your patterns of driving, the stores where you shop, and the people you see regularly can all be subject to change. The farther away you move, the more difficult the transition.

Saying good-bye through ritual can affirm relationships on a heart-felt level by honoring the people who have meant the most to you. It can create room to release the emotions that may be rising and cresting as you take time to adjust, grieve, and let go. The rite helps to integrate changes with more ease. It gives you an opportunity to release and mitigate some of the stress, mourning the past and embracing the future. Look at the land around your home and share with those you live with a story you recall about the outdoors of your home. With an imaginary spiral, circle into the house from outside. Then, starting with the front door, go from room to room and tell a story about something you remember from there. You might want to light a candle and walk together, or go arm in arm from room to room. You can say a prayer of thanksgiving for each room, or leave a flower on the windowsill as you say good-bye.

If you are moving in, you can burn sage and cedar in a shell or bowl in each room to clean out the energy of the people who were there before and bring in more love, respect, trust, or whatever you choose to bring into your new home. Be sure to include the children. Close with a prayer for the family or blessing of the house. If the energy in your new place is really negative, you may want to use salt mixed with water instead of sage and say prayers bringing in the archangels to stand at the four corners of your house. They are Michael, Gabriel, Ariel, and Rafael.

MAY **29**, **Focus**. *I give myself the gift of focus in my work and life. Where does resistance surface? What are the challenges that I face?*

MAY **30**, **Silence**. *I seek the healing balm of silence to rejuvenate me and heal the places I need to rest in order to restore myself.*

～～ Memorial Day ～～

The last Monday in May is annually set aside to remember those who died during wars in which the United States has fought. Parades and flowers on graves of loved ones, whether military or not, are the common observances. In many seaports, flowers are also released onto the water.

Have you lost someone, whether through war, violence, or a peaceful ending? Take today to remember them, either with flowers placed on their graveside, or by visiting a place where you spent some time together. Go with a friend or loved one and tell a story of what you remember about the person you lost.

MAY **31**, **Budding**. *As May brings buds and new flowering, I am blossoming into more of myself. All is well.*

Today, honor what is budding in you with the following spring salad dressing recipe, which my mother, Martha, taught me, probably taught to her by my grandmother. I have added my own variations to it. It goes well on anything from green salads to fruit salad.

Martha's Marvelous Salad Dressing
1 garlic clove
1 tablespoon salt
1 tablespoon dried and/or fresh basil, tarragon, dill, oregano, or marjoram, use one herb as dominant and two as subordinate flavors in lesser amounts.
½ to ¼ cup vinegar
½ cup sherry or wine
½ cup olive oil

With a fork, mash the garlic clove into the salt and herbs until a lumpy paste develops. Pour in the vinegar stirring vigorously. Add the wine and the olive oil to taste. Mix well before you pour onto the salad. (For extra zest add curry or turmeric depending on what you are cooking, either of them adds a special flavor.)

〜〜 Spring Bath 〜〜

In a sachet or piece of cotton, add some sprigs of marjoram, sage, rosemary, a clove, and a cinnamon stick. Tie up the bundle with a string or ribbon and float it in your bath like a giant tea bag. Or try sandalwood as an alternative to the spices. Light a candle and soak!

June

Earth and Heaven are in us.
—Mahatma Gandhi

JUNE WAS NAMED AFTER THE ROMAN goddess of marriage, Juno. Juno is the goddess who watches over women, and that's why June is the month most favorable for marriage. June was also the month dedicated to young men in Rome. Some people believe the name came from the Latin word for young men, *juniors*. However, since the original name for June is *Junonius*, it's more likely named after the Roman queen of heaven, who corresponds to Mary in the Christian tradition, Frigg in the Norse pantheon. While Juno rules the light, she is the counterpart of Janus, who rules at the darkest time of the year. Juno Moneta, who is the guardian of money, had a temple dedicated to her on the Capitoline hill in Rome, which contained the mint where Roman coins were produced.

Brachmanoth, or Bbrak Month, was the name the Franks gave to June, while the backwoods folks call the June full moon the Hot or Strawberry Moon. The gems for June are the agate, pearl, alexandrite, and moonstone. The flower is the rose.

JUNE 1, **Bright.** *I tune to the brightness of the day to inspire and encourage me. Whether there is gloomy weather or not, I am radiant on the inside.*

JUNE 2, **Sun.** *As the sun warms the Earth, I can feel the glow of the sun within me.*

A Relationship Booster

Here is a practice for that moment when you and your partner are ready for a new level of commitment. It acknowledges your willingness to give to one another and sets the tone of respect that is so vital in a relationship.

Separately, make a list of ten things that you would like to receive from the other person: a rose, a compliment, a back rub, and so on. Put the lists on the refrigerator or exchange them. The agreement is to do one a week. When the list is exhausted, either repeat the items or make a fresh list.

JUNE 3, **Exposure.** *The sun exposes the places I need to grow, the challenges ahead, and the limitations I have set forth.*

JUNE 4, **Encouragement.** *I am encouraged to be with the challenges of the day by the light of the sun making everything around me green.*

JUNE 5, **Savor.** *I savor today, knowing that every moment is one of a kind.*

JUNE 6, **Sparkle.** *I watch the sparkle in the air, on the water, and in the eyes of others as I move through my day. Every twinkle reminds me to enjoy life.*

JUNE 7, **Mist.** *Early morning mists help me to see that not everything can be known. I allow the mystery of life to envelop me.*

JUNE 8, **Greening.** *I am greening like the trees and flowers into my blossoming.*

Committing to Yourself

In June the romance of weddings abounds. But have you ever thought of marrying yourself? Since we cannot truly love another unless we love ourselves, why not celebrate your love for yourself with a wedding just for you. Buy a ring that signifies your commitment to yourself. Light a candle, and before you slip the ring on your own finger, try these simple words: "On this day I am committing to love, respect, and trust myself unconditionally and without reservation, through all time and space and into eternity and beyond. As it is spoken, so it is."

JUNE 9, **Energy.** *If I tune into the Earth and the sky, I have unlimited energy.*

JUNE 10, **Innocence.** *The innocence of children gives me a fresh perspective on life. I come to life innocent and new.*

JUNE 11, **Stress.** *I know that a certain amount of stress is good and helps me grow and thrive. I know when I reach my limit and give myself time to relax, rest, and rejuvenate myself.*

JUNE 12, **Details.** *I pay attention to details today, noticing that nature has a place for everything.*

Often we are freed up by taking care of business in every detail, and it is the details in life that make life rich and beautiful. Today, choose to be nourished by the little things in life.

JUNE 13, **Color.** *Today I notice the colors of the day, as bright and as dull as they may be, which make life rich and interesting.*

JUNE 14, **Intensity**. *The sun's intensity matches my own spark of fire within my heart. I allow it to ignite, and I burn with the radiance of my divine spark of fire.*

～～ Father's Day ～～

Every year on the third Sunday in June, folks in the United States and Canada celebrate Father's Day. It was initiated in this country by Sonora Louise Smart Dodd of Spokane, Washington, in 1910. Since it is near the summer solstice, which is often recognized as the time of the masculine principle shining through, it is not a mystery that it should be celebrated at this time of the year.

JUNE 15, **Ferocity**. *I allow myself to feel my ferociousness and express it when necessary. I set my boundaries with ferocity when needed. I remember that nature has a ferocious aspect.*

Blessing the Father and Receiving the Blessing of the Father

If you choose to do the following to honor Father's Day in a group ceremony, it is important to communicate to the group what you would like to do ahead of time. This rite is taken from a book by George Taylor called *Talking with Our Brothers*. It allows you to feel gratitude for the gifts from your father or elders, to feel more gracious in general, and to bless others more easily.

Sitting in a circle, begin by stating your intention and listen to the intentions of others. Imagine together that you are surrounding the circle in gold light. The leader starts by guiding a simple visualization:

"Close your eyes, sit up or lie down, whatever works for you. Breathe slowly in your body. Now let yourself think about the way you have received blessings from your father or another important male elder.

"Focus on one specific event. How did you feel at that time; recall the feeling. What was the sound in his voice, and in yours? Remember the sights and sounds and smells of the interaction. How did you feel? Excited? Scared? Friendly? Were you aware of how you were feeling? What exactly were you receiving? Acknowledgement for what? Could you fully receive this gift?

"Take some time now to bring your father or an elder into your heart and thank him for caring. Let yourself feel what he was feeling as he reached out to you. See yourself as he must have seen you. Feel his generous praise and love.

"Whether he is dead or alive, let yourself express the gratitude you have for him. Offer a prayer or blessing to him.

"Now let go of the man in your heart. Say good-bye to him in some way.

"Bring yourself back into the room, feel your body and feet on the floor. Take several minutes to share feelings and memories."

Some folks may want to follow up this exercise with a visit or a call to their mentor or father figure. You may want to gather again to share the follow up.

JUNE 16, **Fervor.** *Sometimes I get into a fervor of ideas, emotions and challenges. This is my passion for life being expressed. Before the fervor gets too much, I declare divine order in my life so everything works together like a passionate symphony.*

JUNE 17, **Strain.** *I notice the strain before it fractures me and allow myself to balance with downtime and rest or exercise to release the strain in my life.*

JUNE 18, **Reminiscence.** *Awareness of the past always serves my present circumstances. Living in the past gives me an excuse to miss the present moment.*

〰〰 Body Glow 〰〰

Buy yourself a new loofa sponge, back brush, or wash cloth, and give yourself a full body scrub in the tub or shower today. Try using Dr. Bronner's peppermint soap for an extra special rejuvenating feeling. Add orange or tangerine rind to the soap for a special, sunny, pick-me-up rub.

JUNE 19, **Glow.** *Today, for just a moment, I watch the glow of sunrise or sunset, knowing there will not be another one like this ever again.*

JUNE 20, **Radiance.** *I look for radiance in others. I feel the sun bursting brightly in my heart.*

6

Summer:
Season of Growth
and Light

*You are what your deep driving desire is. As your
desire is, so is your will. As your will is, so is your
deed. As your deed, so is your destiny.*

—The Upanishads

DIRECTION: East, Sun

ASTROLOGICAL SIGNS:

Cancer: June 21–July 22   *Leo:* July 23–August 22
Virgo: August 23–September 22

AHH, SUMMER! The time of heat, sun, and rain to nourish the plants and animals, the blossoming trees and growing plants, and the fullness of the Earth in all her splendor, fostered by the light of the sun. Represented by the color yellow for sunshine, summer begins on the solstice, June 21, the longest day of the year.

The Native American people from the southwest to the great plains hold various ceremonies in honor of the sun. The Aztecs, Mayan, and Incas held ceremonies for the sun gods and temple pyramids. On other continents, summer offers celebrations for growth and harvest.

In Japan, people climb Mount Fuji for two months in the summer when there is no snow. In Europe, June 21 marks summer solstice rituals, which are enacted at sacred sites. Stonehenge, for example, was the site of Druid practices, until vandals and unruly spectators closed direct access to the stones.

In western culture, summer is the time for vacations and play, for being out of doors, and for relishing the long summer nights.

～～ Symbols and Key Words for Summer ～～

East, transformation, new beginnings, the masculine principle, logic, what can be seen, rising sun, heat, fire, the color yellow. A snake, candle, or yellow cloth can symbolize this direction.

JUNE 21, **Light.** *Today I enjoy every minute of the longest daylight of the year. I open to what is revealed for me today by the sun's rays.*

JUNE 22, **Mystery.** *Today, I am aware of mystery—in me, through me, and with me. I am aware of how I might limit the unknown by the concrete. I am willing to experience the mystery of life.*

JUNE 23, **Feet.** *My feet walk on the back of Mother Earth. She is there for me with every step. I am grateful for my feet, which carry me everywhere. I am nurtured by the Earth through the foods I eat. All is well.*

Take some time to notice your connection to the Earth through your feet and through your connection through an invisible umbilical cord that moves from the base of your spine into the Earth.

～～ Body Image Ritual ～～

Summer is the time of bathing suits and fewer clothes. Many people, especially women, spend much of their summers hating their bodies. Today, take time to really look at yourself in the mirror. Write down a list of all the parts that you dislike on your body or circle them on a full-length mirror in lipstick or washable marker. Go through them one by one and write down your complaints next to the part. Then over the negative thoughts write: cancel, cancel. Now write under the body part: "You are beautiful like the Goddess. You are beautiful; you are a sacrament." If you cannot convince yourself that you are beautiful just the way you are, have a conversation with that part and ask it why it is not the shape you want it to be. Really listen!

Your body will answer you. Keep working with the parts that you do not love until you can love yourself completely, just as you are.

JUNE 24, **Presence.** *My presence is the biggest gift I have been given. I allow myself to be present fully as I move through my day.*

JUNE 25, **Dance.** *I let life move through me in my dance today.*

What if you danced through this day? Imagine how differently the day would unfold.

JUNE 26, **Earth.** *Today I notice the mystery of the Earth, even under the cement of the city, I am walking on the Earth. I feel her pulse and remember that she is a living being.*

Honoring Personal Transitions

When you have just given birth, given away your daughter in marriage, begun menopause, or retired, you are in the midst of major transition. It's a shift in relationship to yourself and your family. In order to incorporate such deep changes on a soul level, it's important to have a transition ceremony. Take some time to ask yourself the following questions:

1. What is it that I really need, now that this part of my life is over? Make a list.

2. How do I really feel? You may want to write in a journal your true feelings—about the wedding, your new life, and so on. You need not share it with anyone, just express it; that is enough.

3. Take your list of needs and begin doing them. If you set your intention to include each item on your list as part of a rite, anything can become part of your transition ritual. Here are some suggestions: Get a massage or get your hair or nails done, and let your massage therapist, hairdresser, or manicurist know that you are recovering from a particular event; that way she can be more supportive during your appointment. Spend a few days alone, with a friend, or with your spouse. Set your intention to celebrate a new beginning with a special dinner with your mate or a friend.

   Ask one or more friends to witness your rite. You may also want to make this a rite with your husband or partner. You could start by drawing a circle of love around you, symbolized by dried rose petals or burning sage or incense.

   Your rite can incorporate journal entries or a letter to your child, God, or your higher power about what you are learning as a part of the transition. You can also include several items on your list of needs. State what you want for the next part of your life. You may include career directions, things you want to do that are new to you, or places in your inner life that you have yet to discover.

   Ask your friends for help. You may want to ask for a foot rub or head massage as a part. Close your rite by touching your heart and head with rose water to bless yourself, or ask a friend or your husband to do this for you. You can also take turns blessing one another.

4. Give yourself some time. Any major transition requires time for recovery. Big changes always imply loss, even with the most joyful events. When you give yourself time to feel the transition, you help yourself take the first steps on your new life path.

JUNE 27, **Song.** *What song will I sing today to stir me? I let my song emerge from my heart. Life is more beautiful if I allow myself to sing.*

JUNE 28, **Hands.** *My hands are the tools that have been given me as extensions of my heart. I notice what they touch and where my hands rest.*

Career Change Ritual

Summer is a time for the masculine principle of being out in the world, a perfect time to sort out your career choices. If you feel it is time for a change, your career will largely determine the components of the ritual as well as the symbols of your career that seem appropriate. The objects you choose can also represent the inner qualities that you want to emphasize as you go through this time of change. For example: A candle represents inner knowing and awareness; water symbolizes cleansing and flow, and so on. The important questions to ask yourself are:

1. What are you letting go of? What do you want to do next? If you don't know, ask yourself what you love to do most? Could you make a living at it? Do you want to make a living at it? Talk to people who are doing what you want to do to see if the direction you are contemplating really suits you. Are there aspects of yourself that need to be listened to and transformed before you make this transition? Perhaps there are fears that need to be addressed or parts of yourself that need reassuring. As you work toward the goal of loving yourself into your new career, the ritual will, in part, create itself.

2. When you have listened to your needs and begun to act on them, you can address other questions such as: How much money do you

want to make? What kind of day do you want to have? How will this new direction contribute to others, the Earth, myself, and my family?

3. Consider symbols of the past and the future. These could be files, pictures, slides of where you have been, items from your desk, photos of what you want to be doing, and so on. Then invite the guests.

4. In the actual ritual, lay out the symbols of the past and choose which ones you want to carry forward into the future. Place what is left in the trash or in storage.

5. Then lay out the symbols for your future and spend a little time integrating them with the things from the past that remain. You can play music and narrate what they mean to you while your friends witness and support your transition. You can glue them on a poster board or arrange them symbolically for your guests to witness.

6. When the change is complete, ask those invited to bless your chosen work.

JUNE 29, **Echo.** *The echo of my life is reflected in everything I do and say. I am grateful for the moments of that reflection. I allow myself time to listen to others.*

JUNE 30, **Inspiring.** *I am inspired to new awareness of the trees, of the grass, and of this season of the sun. I let nature inspire me. All is well.*

Supporting Children's Changes

Part of living a sacred life is supporting those around us, particularly the young ones. Their transitions from childhood to adulthood come in stages, from their first adult action in adolescence until they leave home. At every stage there is something you can do to honor their changes.

For a child's first adult action, such as taking out the garbage without being asked, cleaning up their dishes, clearing the table without being prompted, or taking responsibility for themselves or some aspect of family life without being told, prepare a special dinner in his or her honor. Let them know you noticed and give them something that has meaning to them. It doesn't have to be an elaborate gift, just meaningful. For early adolescents and graduates, see the index.

July

It does not require many words to speak the truth.
—Chief Joseph, Nez Perce

THE SEVENTH MONTH WAS ORIGINALLY the fifth month on the Roman calendar. They named it *Quintilis*, which means fifth. Julius Caesar gave the month thirty-one days and the Roman senate named it *Julius* in honor of their Caesar. Known as the month of the Buck Moon in the backwoods American tradition, July is called *Iuil* by the Irish, another name for Julius. The Anglo-Saxons called it *Aeftera Litha*, meaning after the summer solstice; they also called it *Maedmonat*, or Meadow Month, referring to the stage of growth the fields are in at this time. *Hewimanoth*, or Hay Month, is the Frankish name for July, referring to hay cutting. The gem for July is the ruby, and the flower is the water lily.

JULY 1, **Honoring the God/Goddess Within.** *I am willing to be seen in the light of the sun. I know that in my heart of hearts I am a spark of divine fire that lives in alignment with the Universe and the changes of the seasons. I can acknowledge this and develop a relationship with this part of myself. All is well.*

Sun Blessing
Acknowledgement is so needed. Women need it from men, and men need it from women. Children need it from everyone.

In this blessing, adapted from a group led by Brenda Morgan, Ph.D., and a book by George M. Taylor, called *Talking with Our Brothers*, people gather to acknowledge one another within a group where trust has been established. It is especially significant when men and women do this exercise together. Only one other person is necessary to do this effectively, however, so if you can't muster a group, try a friend or two. The impact of the larger group can be a revelation, so choose this option if possible.

1. Gather a group of friends together in a semicircle. Let people know what you are doing before you invite them.

2. Invite one person to stand or sit in the center of the group.

3. The person in the center begins to speak of his or her own positive qualities, attributes, talents, or gifts. What does she love about herself? What does he see as his contribution to the world?

4. The group's job is to render feedback as to the sincerity and honesty of the person. If the person is not felt to be honest or true enough, then the group has the person in the center do this over again until authenticity is felt.

5. Then each person in the semicircle affirms the person in the center in their own way, by naming the gifts they see in the person at hand. Each person in the group takes turns sitting in the center and being the radiant sun.

6. A variation of this exercise focuses on singing the name of the person. The person sings, "I am Mara . . ." Then the group sings back the name in unison to the person.

～～ Royal Pillow Day ～～

When was the last time you treated yourself like a queen or a king and laid around in bed all day pampering yourself? Take a day off from work or spend a weekend day in bed. Do nothing but self-pampering—hair, nails, massage, eating good food, reading trashy (or good) novels, watching old movies, or whatever you choose.

JULY 2, **Slowing Down.** *I allow my inner heart to match the outer one. I slow down enough to feel how I move through my day.*

JULY 3, **Inspire.** *Today I allow myself to be inspired and to expand into more awareness of love all around me.*

Your Personal Mission Statement

Within the word inspire are the words *spire*, to move up, and *in*, or to evolve. To move from divine inspiration is to move up within our awareness of something larger, something beyond our current thoughts. When we do so, we are actually moving closer to the Spirit. Today, think of what inspires you in life. Is it a person, a song, a phrase, an idea? Write it down and put it somewhere so you can see it often—on your computer, the phone receiver, your mirror, or on the dashboard of your car.

JULY 4, **Celebrate.** *Today I find more and more to celebrate in my life. I see my burdens as gifts, and I see my troubles as challenges. I can understand the* *lessons more clearly so I need not repeat them again. I choose to celebrate life rather than diminish it.*

To celebrate Independence Day, try this luscious cheesecake, a treat for body and soul.

Aunt Susan's Chocolate Tofu Cheesecake
Crust:
⅓ box Chocolate Nilla Wafers, crushed
6 tablespoons butter or margarine, melted

Filling:
1 8-ounce package cream cheese
1 10–12 ounce package soft tofu
½ cup whipping cream
½ cup sugar
6 ounces semisweet chocolate, melted
4 eggs
1 teaspoon vanilla
1 teaspoon grated orange rind or 2 teaspoons orange extract
   (optional)

Preheat the oven to 325 degrees. Make the crust by mixing together the wafer crumbs and butter or margarine, then press them on the bottom and up the sides of an 8-inch pie pan.

Using a food processor, blend together cream cheese and tofu. Add whipping cream and sugar; blend until smooth. Blend in melted chocolate, then eggs, vanilla, and orange rind or extract, if desired. Pour into prepared pan. Bake for one hour or until set. Test with toothpick. Let cool and chill.

Serve with whipped cream if desired, garnished with extra orange rind. Serves 6–8.

JULY 5, **Honesty.** *Honesty is the cornerstone of trust in relationships. If I cannot be honest with myself, then I cannot be honest with others. I look within for the truth which sets me free from limitation and mistrust.*

JULY 6, **Honor.** *Today I honor the fact that everyone's lessons and challenges are different.*

Loving the Differences

Each of us is unique, and the differences in your children or your lover or your best friend make the world a much richer place. Although we know this, it is sometimes hard to put it into practice. When you honor another's path, however, you can honor where they are and honor your own journey at the same time. In this way, we develop more respect for the other's path and we can share those lessons that we learn along the way with more understanding.

Here is an exercise to help. Take a few deep breaths as you sit comfortably. Visualize yourself being in a bubble of colorful light. Now see your child or mate in their bubble. It will have its own color, shape, and size. See the bubbles as distinct and different. Let your wonder and childlike curiosity observe the differences and appreciate them. Do not try to change or manipulate their bubble in anyway. When you have completed, thank them and release them, coming back into your bubble, into your breath, and into your heart, returning with full consciousness.

〰〰   **Personal Power Standing Meditation**   〰〰

Stand in an upright position with your feet shoulder-width apart. Take several deep breaths to help you relax. Bend your knees slightly so that your lower back is flat, then tilt the front of your hips toward your back. Concentrate on your breathing. Allow yourself to breathe freely, counting from one to ten, then starting again at one. Notice how relaxed and still you can be at the same time. If you start to tense up, in your shoulders, in your back or neck, just breathe into that area, move your head or shoulders slightly and they will uncoil. Spend five, ten, fifteen, or twenty minutes in this posture—whatever is comfortable for you.

JULY 7, **Responsibility.** *Part of moving into the new consciousness of love and peace is taking responsibility for our thoughts and feelings.*

Form Follows Your Thought

Have you ever noticed that perhaps a few months earlier you thought something, and then without noticing, you were doing what you had been thinking about? We all manufacture thoughts that lay out our future in front of us at such a rate that we are barely conscious of what we are doing. If we remember that form follows thought, we can become more aware of how our thinking truly creates our reality. Then we can begin to take charge of our life by taking responsibility for our thinking. You can cancel thoughts you don't like as easily as you make them, by imagining a cancel stamp over a thought as soon as you think it. For example, the thought, My nose looks ugly. You can cancel that and correct your thought pattern, My nose is unique and beautiful. I love my nose.

Here is another idea: Imagine what you would really like in your life, something within your grasp. Now take a moment and be grateful for what you have already received. Then set your intention to receive what you are asking for by writing it down on a piece of paper or by drawing yourself into the picture of what you would like. Let yourself have it in your mind. Now put the drawing or letter away. Imagine you can release this thought completely in a hot air balloon to the Spirit without another thought. Let it be for at least a full moon cycle.

JULY 8, Vulnerable. *Being vulnerable with those who are closest to you is the gateway to more compassion, trust, and love.*

JULY 9, Intimate. *When I am vulnerable more intimacy forms.*

Deepening Your Connections

Intimacy and vulnerability go hand in hand. When you allow time and space to be with someone, you can reach new levels of intimacy. And when we are vulnerable, we are showing the truth of our feelings in the moment.

Here is an exercise that can help: Sit with your partner or a friend. Take turns really listening to each other. Express something to your partner that you may not have said before. It could also be something about yourself that you have not shared but want him or her to know. You can also ask her/him for something you would like to receive—support, an ear massage, time away—whatever may be important to you. To increase your contact, hold hands. Listen and receive, speak and be heard, feel the other really appreciating you. Take as long as you need.

～～ Balancing Time ～～

Take a piece of paper and fold it in quarters, then open it again. At the top of one quarter, write self, on the top of the opposite side, write others. Then go over your day and write down what you have done that day for yourself or for others. You can include activities with physical manifestations, such as helping with your child's homework or exercising, and private activities, such as meditation, listening to music, or whatever crosses your mind. Then take a moment and look at your list. Is it balanced between the two? Then try to sense whether or not you feel balanced. If not, what is it that you need to correct the imbalance? Remember, you can give to others while you give to yourself. Make a note of which activities you were able to feel yourself give to both yourself and another person at the same time.

JULY 10, **Alone.** *Solitude is a significant component in creativity. When I can be alone with myself, I open to a world of my thoughts, feelings, needs, and ideas.*

JULY 11, **Support**. *Today, I open to receiving support from others when I ask for it. I risk showing my vulnerability by doing so.*

Time for Yourself

When was the last time you took time alone for yourself? All of us need time alone, away from being responsible for others. Being with ourselves is necessary to notice and support what we need in order to be whole, creative, and alive. Plus, when you become aware of your own thoughts, feelings, needs, and ideas, then you can truly be in relationship with others. You can state clearly what support you may need to those who may be willing to provide it.

Here is an exercise you can do anywhere, whether you are on the bus, in the car, or relaxing in bed. Take a deep breath and go into your heart garden. Is it in need of repair, or is it growing and flourishing? Just be with it. If you want to change things, go for it; this is your space. Set your boundaries around the outside and clear out any unwanted energies or people. If it is dark, imagine your wisdom-self bringing in some light. You can invite in your inner child, inner parents, or the male and female aspects of yourself (these may be very different from your actual parents), your power animal, or whatever you choose into your heart garden. Once you are in touch with this space, you will never be without it and can return as often as you like to restore yourself and heal. When you make your heart a sanctuary of love, you find inner peace.

JULY 12, **Radiance**. *I choose to feel radiant today. If I start from the inside out with the light inside my heart, I can move outward to the world, radiating love.*

Ceremonies for Passages

This ritual can be used for anyone who is making a passage, graduation, or transition. Maybe you have a parent who has gone back to school or a child who has just started menstruation. Is there a need for such a rite in your family? Who would be there? Who would be honored? Where would you want to hold the ritual? What kind of object would you use to pass from person to person? How would it look?

In the northwest coast cultures of Native America, potlatches or giveaways were given in honor of children when they were initiated into adulthood. The child received very little of material value. His or her gift was a spiritual one, namely the honor of becoming an adult member of the community. Not only did the child have to prove their practical skills, they also demonstrated their knowledge of the songs, mythology, and blessings that went along with hunting, food gathering, and food preparation. The give away honored the child while giving directly to the community and redistributing the wealth. The wealth and status of the host was measured by his generosity. Sometimes the host even gave away his house.

It is different in our culture. We give a gift to a person. The individual is honored with the gift. Status is in material value and accumulated wealth.

Keep in mind the gift here is a symbolic way to commemorate a moment of crossing into a new time of life. A gift of the heart need not be expensive; indeed a homemade gift often means more.

To perform such a ceremony, gather participants and the object to be given as the gift in a circle. It doesn't matter what kind of an object is used, where the ritual is held, or who is present. The only requirements are willingness between people to express love and caring. The simple format of a circle in which the honoree is in the center helps the honoree stand out. All you do is pass the object from the child to another person, who then expresses his or her hopes, dreams, and good wishes for the child. The object is then passed back to the child and then on to the next person. This helps maintain a focus while symbolically weaving people together. At the end, the object is given to the honoree.

JULY 13, **Frustration.** *Today, I release my frustrations and do what is in front of me to do.*

Going with the Flow

If you get frustrated with a situation, you may be trying to "push the river," or control what is uncontrollable. Often underneath the need to control is a desire for expression, for joy. "If only," often precedes the frustrating thought. When you learn to put those thoughts into a hot air balloon and release them, you can do what is in front of you to do and step into greater peace.

JULY 14, **Liberation.** *Today I look to the areas of my life crying out for liberation and ask what is it that I am wanting more responsibility for in my life.*

Liberation goes hand in hand with responsibility. As you gain freedom, you take more power unto yourself and have more responsibility to create your life.

JULY 15, **Empowerment.** *Today I look at my choices. When I am able to choose, I feel empowered to be who I am.*

Being all of who you are includes the angry parts, the sad parts, and the unacknowledged parts of yourself. Once they are included in your inner family, you can move out in a broader circle and feel joy within for more love, more wholeness, and more compassion.

JULY 16, **Acknowledgement.** *When I acknowledge myself, I can acknowledge others more freely. When I recognize my own abilities and possibilities, I can be at peace with love for myself. Then I can easily extend love and harmony to others.*

JULY 17, **Will.** *When my will is aligned with universal will, I am better able to go with the flow, allow for change, and open myself up to more surprises in life.*

JULY 18, **Surrender.** *When I can open to change, I surrender to the flow of life.*

Surrender does not mean giving up; it means being aware that there is a larger order to life that you are a part of. When you surrender, you recognize that order and humble yourself enough to align your will with Divine will.

Surrender Ritual

For a week every night before going to bed, light a stick of incense and set it in an incense burner, on your altar if you have one, or on a table. As you light the incense, make a commitment to follow Divine will, perhaps with a phrase such as, "not mine, but thine," or "thy will be done," or "from you through me."

JULY **19**, **Growth.** *Like any new growth of a plant or a tree, we go through growing pains.*

Children have physical growing pains and sometimes as adults we have them in the form of an accident, a fall, or an illness. It may be helpful to see how these incidents fit into the rest of our lives and our story. We can view the situation and pay attention to any potential lessons. Then we can be free to cooperate with the growth that is calling to us.

JULY **20**, **Expansion.** *Today I take a moment and look with an eagle's view on my life.*

If we think of expansion as a bigger view, we can imagine for a moment that we are looking from the eyes of an eagle. How different life looks from there!

JULY **21**, **Conflicts.** *Today I choose to let my conflicts teach me about the lessons I need to learn.*

How are the conflicts in your life serving you? The question can be answered simply and easily if you remember to ask yourself: How is this person or aspect of myself helping me to grow?

JULY **22**, **Detachment.** *Today I view with detachment the activities that swirl around me and rest in peace for a moment of reflection.*

There are situations where detachment is required and helpful. It gives us an opportunity to be aware of a broader view and to disengage emotionally from conflict that is not serving anyone.

JULY 23, **Attachment.** *Today I release attachments by respectfully drawing back my energy. I allow myself to feel the freedom of choice, and I love without attachment.*

Sometimes we feel the strings of attachment to a place or person almost as if we were attached by a cord. While attachments are necessary in some circumstances, say with small children, most attachments are lines of our energy that serve only to siphon our strength and are unnecessary. Attachment is not love.

JULY 24, **Freedom.** *Today I allow myself to be free in my choices and know that if my beliefs create boundaries for me, then I have made a choice in advance. I can make a different choice or adjust my belief if I choose.*

Many people think that being free has to do with mobility. Although being unattached allows freedom on one level, true freedom is an inside reality. It is knowing that we have choices at all times. We can choose to react, act, or be silent. Every choice we make has a cause and effect, which occur and are influenced by our beliefs and expectations.

∼∼ In Service to the Earth ∼∼

The following meditation is inspired by Sue Patton Thoele's, The Woman's Book of Spirit: In your mind's eye, imagine that you are going to your favorite place on the breast of Grandmother Earth. Let yourself feel her beauty, wildness, and power. Ask her what it is that she needs from you to assist her. Listen to her answer in the trees, on the wind, in your heart.

JULY 25, **Faith.** *My trust is strong when I can allow the unfolding of a greater plan to emerge. I trust that my part is unfolding.*

JULY 26, **Enjoyment.** *Play is as important as anything to rebalance our lives and help us experience more joy. Today I look for the joy in everything I do, and I find it!*

JULY 27, **Fun.** *Today I let my inner child be playful. I find something to laugh about, something to hold lightly and bring a new perspective to my life.*

Fun is an important aspect of being one with the Spirit. When was the last time you really played?

JULY 28, **Flow.** *Today I relax in the flow of life, letting go of plans if need be to honor the direction of my life. Sometimes life takes us in a different direction than we planned. When this happens, and you choose not resist it but rather to go with it, you are in the flow.*

JULY 29, **Limits.** *Today I set necessary limits with my loved ones and with my relationship as a message of self-respect. I am aware of my limits, and I honor them.*

Setting limits with others can be a way of deepening our self-understanding. When we set limits, we are saying to another that this is where my energy stops toward you, and this is where I need to be met.

JULY 30, **Triggers.** *Today I look at my triggers. I know that where I am triggered I have a wound.*

What is triggering your emotions in reaction to circumstances around you? When you take time to focus on the source of the trigger, breathing into your body where the wound is held, you can transform this wound into more love and harmony within.

JULY 31, **Honesty.** *When I share honestly, I am seen and heard by those I trust.*

Sometimes the hardest thing to do is to be honest. Honest feedback is an investment of energy in a relationship. When we speak honestly, we hope that the other person will hear us and receive our feelings with an open mind. The way that we deliver honest insight can make all the difference.

August

[W]isdom comes only when you stop
looking for it and start truly living the life
the Creator intended for you.

—Leila Fisher, Hoh Elder,
Northwest Coast

DEMETER, WHO IS GODDESS OF THE HARVEST, was honored by the Romans during August, which was named after the first Roman emperor, Augustus Caesar. This month is known in the Celtic traditions as *Lughnassadh*, or *Lunasa*, from the Celtic god of wisdom, *Lugh*, the deity of London and Lyons. (Odin, from Norse mythology is comparable to Lugh.) The first day of August is still celebrated as the Lammas festival in the Celtic tradition. Tradition has it that the first corn is cut, baked into a loaf, and offered to Lugh in thanksgiving. August is known as the Corn Moon or the Sturgeon Moon in backwoods traditions of the United States, which may have originated from the Franks, who called it the Corn Ears Month or *Aranmanoth*.

For many Americans, August is the time of summer vacations, golden wheat fields, ripe sweet corn, and the beginning of the harvest. August gems are peridot and sardonyx; the flowers are poppy and gladiolus.

〜〜 Ritual of Appreciation 〜〜

From a book called Simple Pleasures *comes a ritual you can do anywhere—at home, in the office, or with kids who tend to hear nothing but complaints from adults.*

Stand or sit in a circle. Choose one person as the focus, and then everyone else, as the spirit moves them, speaks on what they appreciate about that person. When everyone has spoken, move onto the next person. There are four rules: remarks must be positive (no sarcasm, backhanded compliments, and so on), no one else may interject anything while someone is speaking, no one has to speak if they don't want to, and the object of the appreciations may not say anything, just take in the praise. (It's surprising how difficult the latter is. But you'll get used to it.)

AUGUST 1, **Strength**. *My strength comes in developing the ability to express myself honestly.*

It takes strength to be true to ourselves. When you express your truth, it may not look anything like you planned. Sometimes it comes out with tears, sometimes with laughter, sometimes forceful or gentle. As we cultivate our inner truth, however, we find the strength to speak it.

AUGUST 2, **Guilt**. *Today I release guilt, knowing that it is only a control mechanism others use or I have learned to use on myself.*

You do not have to respond to guilt trips that others choose to administer. When we are released from guilt, we are free to respond according to our free will.

AUGUST 3, **Values.** *Today I am aware of my values as the guideposts of my life. I live by the guideposts of the culture and my own values.*

Clarifying Your Values

Before street signs were developed, guideposts were found at intersections of roads to help travelers on their way. In such a way, our values guide us through our lives. Some are passed down through our families; others are a natural evolution of what is true for us. At some point, it is wise to review our values, both inherited and those we have stumbled upon ourselves, to see what truly works. In your journal or on a sheet of paper, make two columns, one that reads "family," and another that says "self." List the sayings, beliefs, and values you are aware of that your family passed down. It could be a common statement such as, "Many hands make less work," or something unique to your family, such as, "Nice people don't express their feelings." On the other side, write the things that you personally value. Now look at the list again and cross out any you don't agree with. Take what remains and write them down on a new sheet. You can also do this with your mate or family members and compare notes.

AUGUST 4, **Withholding.** *Today I am present to any areas in my life where I am withholding, and I release what is appropriate for me.*

AUGUST 5, **Perspective.** *Today I look at others' perspective and share my own perspective to gain better understanding of all sides of an issue.*

Clarifying Your Beliefs

Beliefs are different than values in one simple way: Values are what you hold dear, and beliefs are statements about the values that you form. While you may value work, for example, your belief may be that you have to work all the time to survive. When we do not change our beliefs from childhood, sometimes they can restrict us to the powerless state we may have experienced as a child.

Ask yourself, "How am I holding back from my life and relationships?" Then ask, "What am I storing that energy for?" Wherever you notice withholding, you notice your limiting beliefs, most likely an outmoded habit learned as a child.

Sometimes personal challenges shift our perspective and help us look at our beliefs. Here is an exercise you can do to look at your unconscious beliefs without an inner earthquake:

1. In a journal or notebook, write down three things a parent always said to you. Don't think about it, just write it down. To help you, imagine you are talking about work, play, fun, creativity, joy, or whatever you choose with your parents and listen to their advice.

2. Write the phrases in quotes so you can be objective about their beliefs.

3. Now really look at it. Take the words apart, take your time to really be with the statements. Do they apply to you today? Is

this really what you want influencing your life? If so fine, if not, write what is true for you and reduce it to a single statement, such as "I believe..."

4. Take a moment to appreciate where your parents came from, the struggles they had, and the parents who raised them. See your life for a moment in the same manner. Notice how everyone has their own perspective even when they are viewing the same situation. Like the story of the blind men who each describe something different when they are touching different parts of the same elephant, we often see things from only one perspective.

5. Share your views with someone you respect to help you describe the differences and similarities of beliefs from you and your family. Even if that person does not agree with your perspective, listen and sort out what is true for you. Feedback from another source helps you uncover more information, and allows you to bring it to awareness.

AUGUST 6, Power. *I look at an area where I can love myself more and feel the power of love in my life.*

Sharing power is a new concept that has evolved only recently. To share power we have to first feel powerful in ourselves. We all need self-esteem, in order to regard ourselves in a positive way. But feeling powerful from an ego view is different than feeling self-love, self-respect, and self-trust.

AUGUST 7, **Prayer.** *Today I ask, believing in the right outcome. If I ask with intention to receive my highest good and release the outcome to the greater universal design, all my prayers are answered. I give thanks for what I have.*

AUGUST 8, **Risks.** *All my risks extend me into the unknown, and I step out on faith, knowing the Universe will respond to my faith.*

Every time you choose to risk, you loosen a little fear and grow a little more. When you choose not to risk, perhaps you are valuing security over challenge. This may be fine. You may be weighing all the factors wisely. However, you may be choosing fear over love. The choice is always yours to make.

Releasing Fears

Here is a little rite you can do to look at your fears. First, make two columns on a sheet of paper or in your journal. Then make a list of what fears pertain to relationship, career, or whatever comes up first. Now in the second column, write down what purpose they serve in your life. Then contemplate the list. Does it change your relationship to your fears?

AUGUST 9, **Peace.** *Inside me is a place where I can rest and relax. I can be crazy, I can be loving, I can be me. Today I rest near the still pool in my heart and find peace.*

AUGUST 10, **Clarity.** *I am open to more clarity in my life and am honest with myself in order to receive the clarity I seek.*

Let the summer sun remind us to let the light of truth shine on our lives. Clarity gives us clear choices to take right action.

AUGUST 11, **Harvest.** *Today I reflect on the harvest. I am open to sufficient supply and sharing the abundance with others.*

AUGUST 12, **Abundance.** *Today I am aware of my abundant gifts, and I honor my creativity.*

Such gifts the Earth offers us at this time of year! When we are in tune with the harvest, we are in tune with one of the cycles of life.

Give Away Time

This abundant time of year is often a good occasion to give things away that you no longer need. You can also give time or talents to those people or organizations that could use your help. During the lazy days of August, think of continuing the cycle of giving and receiving by holding a ritual giveaway. Make it an annual event if you wish. The gifts should be things that you really cherish, not garage sale items. Although a good garage sale goes a long way in clearing your home of unnecessary items.

AUGUST 13, **Awareness.** *Today I open my heart to perceive with love the actions of others.*

The more aware you can be, the more you can understand yourself and others. You make clearer choices. You become more aware of a plan that is greater than you can imagine.

AUGUST 14, **Balance.** *Today I rest in balance, knowing that my balance point changes as I grow and change. I welcome balance as a place to begin anew.*

When you bring balance to your life, it is often from an out of balance place. When you are aware of what is balanced, you can test the water of your edges to gain perspective on what the truth is for you.

AUGUST 15, **Guidance.** *Today I am guided for my highest good and the good of others. Everything is in divine order.*

AUGUST 16, **Telling the Truth.** *When I speak my truth, without blame or judgment, I am honoring others while I respect myself. Today I tell the truth.*

AUGUST 17, **Asking for What We Want.** *Today I exercise asking, so that I might receive.*

The hardest thing for some of us is to ask for what we want. When you ask for what you want, you are appearing in the moment with a request that someone just might be able to fulfill. You also risk the possibility of there not being someone to meet your needs. But whether or not they can fulfill it, asking opens you up to vulnerability and that is a place God can enter your life.

AUGUST 18, **Points.** *Today I release the past and release the points of pain in my body by sending a message of love to those areas.*

Body Scan for Better Health

Our body has points that the Chinese call meridians. These points correspond to various organs and run from the top of our head down our arms and legs to our fingers and feet. When we have a point of pain in our system, we are being told that something is out of balance. The same is true in our lives. When we come to a point of pain, we are being asked to release the pain or release the past memories or beliefs that we are out-growing.

Try this exercise to help yourself release tender points. Lay down on a comfortable surface. Take three deep breaths to relax you. Scan your body with your inner awareness, from the top of your head to the tips of your toes. When you feel a point of pain or feel tension breathe into that place until it releases, holding the intention of it relaxing. Take your time. Don't rush. This is especially good when you come home from work and want some transition time.

AUGUST **19**, **Direction.** *I honor the flow of my life and the directions that lead me to new understandings. I surrender to the direction my life wants to take.*

Our society calls us to make plans, to know where we are going, and to work systematically to get there. Usually, however, the natural flow of life is not a straight line, but one of cycles and spirals. So take some time today to recognize the shape of the flow of your life.

AUGUST **20**, **Goals.** *Today I make plans, knowing they can change at any moment, teaching me over and over to let go and let God.*

There is a saying, "If you want to make God/Goddess laugh, show her/him your plans." We need to plan, but we need to be willing to change plans as life moves through us.

The Miracle of Miracles

On August 20, 1994, a white buffalo calf was born on the Heider farm in Janesville, Wisconsin, and was named, appropriately, Miracle. Her birth fulfills a longstanding Native American prophecy about the return of White Buffalo Calf Woman. She was a mystical woman who brought the Ancient Lakota Sioux traditions and customs to the people after a period of starvation and despair. It is believed by many indigenous people that the birth of this calf, the first one born in sixty-one years, ushers in a time of peace and renewed faith in life.

AUGUST 21, **Path.** *My path unfolds before me. All is well.*

If you can see down the road only a short distance, this is enough and good, because everything moves in coordination with every other living thing in the cosmos. Our thoughts form our reality, and if our thoughts are moving slowly, this is good. We are being deliberate about our chosen path.

AUGUST 22, **Harmony.** *Everything is in harmony and divine order. Everything is in concert, and I rest in the knowledge that I know my part and play in harmony.*

When you declare divine order for yourself, then you have the chance to sing, to be with all that is happening beyond your world. If there are apparent delays, perhaps the information you have received so far is incomplete. You need only expand into a greater awareness.

AUGUST 23, **Acknowledgement.** *Today I acknowledge something in myself that I have not yet recognized. I am at peace.*

AUGUST 24, **Request**. *My requests can be revealed with ease and wonder. If I ask the Universe for help, knowing the help will come, it will. My sincere requests are answered. Then it is up to me to do my part when the answer comes.*

AUGUST 25, **Money**. *I notice the flow of energy in my life and ask for what I need.*

Money is a form of energy and offers us an opportunity to show our commitment. Where we put our money, we put our life force. It is a commitment of energy, a conversion of our time into dollars.

AUGUST 26, **Speaking from the Heart**. *Today I speak from my heart.*

When we speak from the heart, our words are always received. When we listen from the heart, we hear levels of awareness that we did not comprehend previously.

AUGUST 27, **Paying Attention**. *Today I pay attention to this moment.*

Being in the present moment is the clay of the future. When we are present to now, we can hear minute details that we might miss otherwise. We can savor those moments with joy.

AUGUST 28, **Letting Go**. *Today I let go of my plan and trust the flow of life.*

AUGUST 29, **Flow**. *Today I am in the flow, life hands me gift after gift, and I am greatly blessed by the new possibilities opening up to me.*

AUGUST 30, **Acceptance**. *Today I accept that my life is a thread in the river of life, and I am grateful and essential to the flow.*

Sometimes it is difficult to grasp the timing of all things beyond our singular lives. If we could see the flow of our lives like a stream of energy, the timing of events, relationships, and all parts of existence that we come in contact with would appear to ebb and flow in a great cosmic soup. Knowing this makes it easier to accept the timing in our own lives.

AUGUST 31, **Actions.** *Today I act according to my heart path, and everything is in right alignment.*

Our actions speak to others of how we walk our talk. What they see is what they get. When our actions are aligned with what we believe and say, then everything we do speaks of power and awareness.

September

Whoever can see through all fear
will always be safe.

—Lao-tzu

NAMED FOR THE ROMAN NUMBER SEVEN, September is also dedicated to the goddess Pomona, who looks after fruit and fruitbearing trees. The Irish call it *Mean Fomair*, the Anglo-Saxons call it Holy Month. Backwoods folks in the United States call it Harvest Moon. The stone for September is the sapphire, the color of trust. The flower is the morning glory.

SEPTEMBER 1, **Fluidity.** *Today I move with fluidity, knowing I am in rhythm with the Universe.*

The Earth's surface is largely made up of water. Our bodies are more than 90 percent water. Our emotions flow like waves when we are upset, happy, or sad. The only certain thing is that our feelings will ebb and flow.

Greek New Year

Since 313 A.D., Greeks have celebrated September 1 as their New Year's Day because it is the beginning of the season for sowing seeds. Although filled with hope and promise, this is also the time when the old people of Greece say that the Angel of Death writes down the names of those who are to die in the year to come, according to *The World Holiday Book.*

Celebrations for the sowing season include blessings of seeds by the local priest, wreath-making of pomegranates, quinces, grapes, garlic, and leaves. The new wreaths are brought to the edge of the sea by the village children just before dawn, along with the old wreaths. The old ones are tossed to the sea, while the new ones are dipped in seawater for luck. Then the tops of forty waves are collected along with forty pebbles and kept in a jar during the coming year, for protection of the harvest and home. Various Greek islands celebrate slightly differently, depending on what they are growing and harvesting. You might want to make a wreath or a flower arrangement for the occasion.

 **Labor Day**

This holiday, celebrated every where in the United States, honors the work force. It was begun in 1882 by Peter J. McGuire, who suggested the holiday to his labor union. The Central Labor Union agreed and staged the first Labor Day in New York's Union Square. Ten thousand people strong, the people celebrated with picnics, fireworks, dancing, and speeches. By 1893, thirty other states had followed New York's lead, and by 1928 all states celebrated Labor Day on the first Monday of September.

What are the contributions you make through your labor? Everyone who works, whether in a job, at home, or in school, is involved in the labor force. You are actually giving your life force to

*work, to yourself, and to other people whom you are serving. Think for
a moment about what you do and recognize yourself for your labor.*

SEPTEMBER 2, **Emotion.** *Today I observe the level of my emotions, like the
waves on the sea. I notice when I am excited, when I am bored, and when
I experience my life force enervated.*

SEPTEMBER 3, **Flexibility.** *Today I notice my flexibility.*

How flexible are you? When does it serve you and when is it a challenge
for you to be flexible? Sometimes we are like willows, sometimes we are
like oaks, and sometimes we are brittle as kindling. Just notice where
you are.

SEPTEMBER 4, **Nourishment.** *Today I focus on nourishment, and I am grateful
for the feast.*

How are you nourishing your body? Are the foods that you take in supporting health or not? What of your soul and heart? How are you feed-
ing them with fun, enjoyment, or inspiration? Take a moment today to
take stock of these vital issues.

SEPTEMBER 5, **The Unknown.** *In the midst of the unknown, I choose to focus
on love.*

All of us face the unknown every time we step out the door. Yet there
are times in our lives that we feel it more poignantly than others.

Especially when we are ill or a loved one is ill, we face the challenge of the unknown. We can take a breather from challenging thoughts of the unknown when we choose to focus on the heart, on love rather than on uncertainty.

〰️ Telephone Meditation 〰️

Before you answer the phone, take a moment to breathe. Vietnamese Buddhist Monk Thich Nhat Hahn suggests you take three breaths before you answer a ringing telephone. The practice brings you back in your body and helps you stay present to the moment, reducing tension. The more the phone rings, the more relaxed and present you will be!

SEPTEMBER 6, **Breath.** *Today I breathe and know that all is well.*

Sometimes the simple act of taking a breath can make a huge difference in our perspective. We can simply breathe, and it brings us back to the moment instead of ahead of ourselves—into the future or the past.

SEPTEMBER 7, **Renew.** *Today I look to what I want to renew and what I want to release.*

Although September is a time of harvest, it is also a time of beginnings. Children and teachers are going back to school, and many of the rest of us see September as the beginning of a cycle.

SEPTEMBER **8**, **Storms.** *Today I focus on the benefit of storms, external and internal for cleaning house.*

The end of summer is the beginning of many storms, which come and go very quickly in many parts of the United States. They deliver rain and blow the dead branches from the trees. Often there is a lot of cleanup after a big storm. I like to think of storms as a way to clean the Earth's house. The fresh air comes in and the old goes out. Old branches are cleaned off, and all the places on our houses that are not nailed down are exposed for repair.

SEPTEMBER **9**, **Intuition.** *Today I listen to my inner knowing and celebrate the wisdom given to me.*

The more we listen to our intuition, the closer we get to our inner wisdom and guidance. It is our internal guide telling us what should be done next. Everyone has it, but not everyone listens to it.

SEPTEMBER **10**, **Harvest.** *Today I look to the harvest and the abundance in my life, and I am grateful.*

SEPTEMBER **11**, **Gratitude.** *Today I give thanks for the things I have. I ask for help and guidance where there is more needed, and I am at peace.*

SEPTEMBER **12**, **Wisdom.** *Today I look for the wisdom that is all around me, in the eyes of others, and in my own heart.*

There is wisdom all around you if only you take the time to look. Nature is full of advice. If you can't get to a wild place, perhaps you can imagine being in the woods where humans have not destroyed the natural rhythms and pathways.

SEPTEMBER 13, **Sharing.** *Today I look to the abundance that I have and find ways to share it with others.*

When we share from our abundance, we create a new economy, one based on plenty—enough for everyone. Try thinking "plenty," instead of "we've got to have," or "there isn't enough."

∿ Rosh Hashanah ∿

This Jewish religious holiday, celebrated on October 2 in 1997, September 21 in 1998, September 11 in 1999, and September 30 in 2000, literally meaning rosh—Head, and Hashanah—the year, or Jewish New Year. During this solemn holiday, Jews begin ten days of penitence, which ends on Yom Kippur, which is the day of atonement. During Rosh Hashanah, Jews pray for forgiveness, a good year, and a long life. The rabbi sounds a ram's horn called the shofar, which calls Jews to repent and reminds people of current affairs that affect Jews. Three sets of prayers are recited during Rosh Hashanah to remind people of God's omnipotence, that God responds to the shofar, and that God remembers deeds.

SEPTEMBER 14, **Charity.** *Today I look with affection on others' faults. I notice how much gentler the world looks from a charitable view.*

The word charity has come to be equated with groups performing good works in the community or donating money. But the word also means kindness in judging other people's faults. The root of the word is from the Latin *caritas* meaning dearness or affection.

SEPTEMBER 15, **Unpredictable.** *Today I am grateful to the unpredictable for adding spice and challenge to life. I am tested by the unpredictable.*

Life is full of unpredictable moments, from the challenging to the surprising. But did you ever imagine what life would be like if everything was known ahead and plans unfolded perfectly every time? How boring life would be.

SEPTEMBER 16, **Flourish.** *Today I give thanks for the areas in my life where I am flourishing.*

What a gift to move beyond survival to thriving. We surge with life when we flourish. There is no stopping the abundant growth and goodwill.

Mexican Independence Day

Celebrated everywhere in Mexico as the day the Mexican Revolution began, September 16 is a more important holiday than Cinco de Mayo, The Fifth of May, which is the day that concludes Mexican independence. Legend has it that on this day in 1810, a priest shouted "Viva la Virgen de Guadalupe!" from his pulpit in Dolores, Guanajuato. The shout spread across Mexico and meant to the people, "Down with Spanish rule! Let Mexicans rule themselves," according to *The World Holiday Book*. The priest, Father Hidalgo, was shot and beheaded for his treason to the Spanish government, and the angry uprising that followed gave way to Mexican independence.

Currently the day is celebrated with feasts, flowers, fireworks, dances, church bells pealing, cockfights, bullfights, and everywhere people shout "Viva la Virgen!"

〰〰 Empower Yourself 〰〰

Take a moment to reflect on the areas in your life where you feel out of control, or where you feel you have no choice. Ask yourself why. Is it that you did not speak up? Has a job or family situation grown out of control? Perhaps you made previous choices that created your present circumstances. Write down what you would like to happen. Then look again at the out of control areas, and brainstorm ways to change these circumstances step by step to your new choice. You may want to get a big sheet of paper and draw your current circumstances on one half of the sheet, what you would like, on the other, and a path between connecting the two. You may have to take baby steps, but each shift along the way will move you from feeling victimized to feeling like you have more autonomy.

SEPTEMBER **17**, **Empower.** *Everyone has the ability to make an impact in their lives or the lives of others each day. Today I empower myself to make a difference by knowing I have choices.*

There is much in our culture that can disempower us if we let it.

When we focus on what we deeply care about, however, it is easy to be empowered to change. We can also support those people who are empowered to do something to make a difference.

SEPTEMBER 18, **Intention.** *When I set my intention with clarity, life unfolds with ease.*

SEPTEMBER 19, **Independence.** *I am self-determining, and the decisions I make, although they may effect others, create my future direction. However, the paradox of my independence rests within the web of everything around me. I am in a stream of life that is connected to everything else on the planet.*

We rely on relationships to sustain us, yet we all long for independence and freedom from time to time. Western culture supports the thoughts that we are independent and have no effect on others as we move through our day. However, everything from economics to home life shows us constantly that this is not the case.

SEPTEMBER 20, **Capture the Moment.** *This is it, the only time we have. Right now—this moment. From here all else follows. The next moment, and then the next. Now . . . Now . . . Now.*

SEPTEMBER 21, **Balance.** *I am balanced in the flow of life, knowing that sometimes finding balance takes some unbalancing. I am challenged to rest and settle in peace into balance.*

SEPTEMBER 22, **Challenge.** *My challenges are grist for the mill. I set myself reasonable challenges that help me grow beyond what I thought possible.*

7

Autumn: Season of Harvest

*Keeping the water pure is one of the first laws
of life. If you destroy the water, you destroy life.*

—Oren Lyons, Onondaga Elder

DIRECTION: West, Water

ASTROLOGICAL SIGNS:

Libra: September: 23–October 22   *Scorpio:* October 23–November 21
Sagittarius: November 22–December 21

DURING AUTUMN, STORMS ONCE AGAIN begin to move over the land. From California fires and earthquakes, to rain and snow in the midwest and east, autumn is a season of changes. It is also a time when the leaves are changing colors and the weather is turning from warm to crisp and cool.

September 23 marks the beginning of the autumnal equinox. Altars or tables of nuts and berries, grapes and corn, squashes and pumpkins, apples and leaves of bright fall colors mark the occasion.

September relates to the time of the visionary in many traditions. The visionary tells the truth without blame or judgment and is also the part of ourselves that sees into the unknown. With nonjudgmental truthfulness, we maintain our authenticity, develop our inner vision, and use our intuition with integrity.

Autumn also relates to the harvest, the gathering of bounty from the year, and the potential for the next year. It is a time of appreciating what we have harvested, and of emptying so we can re-fill.

~~~ **Symbols and Key Words for Autumn** ~~~

The feminine principle; emotions; flexibility; water; fluidity; nourishment; the unknown; the color black; the place where weather comes from, storms and rain; mystery; harvest; abundance; silence; wisdom; water creatures; tears; letting go; trusting; open to right timing and outcome; surrendering the triangle for the feminine prin-ciple, and the mother, maiden, and crone or elder woman, or father, mother, and child; and the circle for coming full circle in the year. A bowl of water and a black or dark blue cloth can be used to sym-bolize this direction.

SEPTEMBER 23, **Hope.** *Today I focus on the moment and what is, gathering my hopes and dreams around me to savor now.*

We all have desires for the future, seeds of promise that we hope will come true. Sometimes giving up hope brings us back into the moment when we can actually do something toward our dreams. When hope borders on expectations, we run the risk of coming up against the reality of what is, rather than what we hoped for.

Autumnal Equinox Celebration

To celebrate this time of year, when the days and nights are of equal length, and the dark begins to overtake the light, gather a group of friends together for a potluck feast (this will save you all the labor and allows oth-ers to share in the celebration). When you are finished with supper, gather in the living room in a circle. You can begin by talking about the waning light and how this night marks the time of the light changing.

The Muskogee Creek people have a story about a spider who wove her web sack to bring back the sun to the Earth. Take a ball of yarn, and holding the end of the yarn, toss it across the circle to someone else. They, in turn, hold on to the end by wrapping it around a wrist or leg, and toss it again to a third person. Make the web of life with the yarn, symbolizing the weaving of night and day, relationships, and the time of autumn. When you are finished, let yourselves be in the web and contemplate the meaning of your connections. Take your time. Don't rush. End by slipping out of the web and noticing the yarn-art you have created together. This is a great rite to do with children.

SEPTEMBER 24, **Uncertainty.** *Today in the face of uncertainty I find assurance in love. When I am faced with uncertainty, I rest in what I know is true and good in my life—the love that I share with those around me, the tasks that I have in front of me, and the love I have for myself within.*

SEPTEMBER 25, **Vision.** *I allow my vision to be what it is. I rest with the knowledge of this inner power.*

Each of us has inner vision. Through our imagination, we expand our dreams and awareness beyond the immediate. When we acknowledge our vision and share it with someone who will value it, we can begin to take action toward our dreams. Sometimes our vision gives rise to thoughts or ways beyond what is apparent in the physical. This is our inner vision at work.

SEPTEMBER 26, **Flow.** *Today I rest with the flow of life and allow the stream to carry me.*

SEPTEMBER 27, **Dance.** *This is the season of the harvest. Many have danced* *in joyful celebration for the harvest during this season. When I dance, I feel the joy of life.*

SEPTEMBER **28, Withdrawing.** *When I withdraw from life, I know it is to gain strength for the next leg of my journey.*

Many people become introverted during the fall. This corresponds to the season when nature begins to withdraw for the winter. Life, which has been abundant, begins to move to plant roots. Animals begin to burrow, storing food and preparing shelter for the long winter. Such feelings are natural.

～～ Autumn Bath-Time Visualization ～～

Draw yourself a bath with a sachet of marjoram and lavender. Both are soothing and cleansing herbs. To make a sachet, simply take a piece of thin cotton cloth, or a piece of fine netting and bundle herbs into it, then tie it with a string or ribbon. It will look like a giant tea bag. Place it in your bath. (It can be used more than once.) Let yourself soak and imagine that you are an animal looking for a place for the winter. You enter the woods or a cavelike area. Silence is all around you. Let yourself nest in a place that is just right for you. Fall into the stillness of the Earth and hear her rhythm. Imagine that you are lying on the Earth like an infant on the tummy of its mother. Let yourself feel held, cradled, and loved by the Earth, knowing you can return to this cave anytime you desire. When you are ready, take a deep breath and come back out of the cave, feeling refreshed and renewed.

SEPTEMBER 29, **Grain**. *Today I give nurturing to the pure potential of love that I am.*

Seeds are potential plants, from redwoods to lettuce leaves. They grow all sorts of amazing foods, and they provide heat and shelter. Love is like water that nurtures the seeds of potential in our hearts. The more we love ourselves, the more we can grow to our full potential, nurturing the love that we are.

Fall Reflection Ritual

Each autumn, our grandparents and great-grandparents would ask themselves: What do I store from this year's harvest? How much? What do I sell? What can I share with my neighbors?

Today life is seemingly more complicated than that. Yet, is it really? Ask yourself: What are the seeds of my life? The ideas, directions I choose, plans, hopes, and dreams? These are the grains of my life that I am constantly planting and reseeding. What is it that I am warehousing? What feelings, thoughts, resentments? Some storage is beneficial, some is contributing to future sabotage.

SEPTEMBER 30, **Storage**. *Today I sort what I have stored away and clean house to prepare for winter.*

How are you storing your surplus? This is a good question to ask in autumn.

Friendship Changes

There are many ways a friendship can change. Moving disrupts relationships, so does changing jobs, even starting in a new position at work. Divorce is another way relationships change, so is starting classes or ending them or getting involved in a new love relationship.

In order to help you process feelings about changes, here is a ritual you can do with a close friend. Talk to your friend first and take time to process your feelings about the friendship. This also lays the groundwork for a successful rite. When you both are ready to begin, find a candle and stand facing each other. Each of you place your hands on the candle. When you are ready, one of you pass the candle around the back of the other falling into an embrace, then, pass it to the other hand and bring it around to the front. Then the other person does the same. When you are finished, you will have made either a figure eight—the symbol of infinity—or a circle—symbolic of the circle you are in together. When you are ready, blow the candle out.

～～ Yom Kippur ～～

The most sacred of the Jewish holidays, Yom Kippur (October 11 in 1997, September 30 in 1998, September 20 in 1999, October 9 in 2000) is the day of atonement for sins. The day is spent fasting and praying, and it occurs ten days after Rosh Hashanah, or the Jewish

New Year. Atonement, really means at-one-ment. Reflect for a moment about ways that you have not been at-one-ment with God. Without indulging in guilt, reflect on ways that you can be at-one-ment, or at peace within yourself with God. Fasting and spending the day in reflection is a good way to spend this day for your peace of mind, or to spark your creativity.

October

Rejoice at your life, for the time is more advanced than you think.

—Chinese proverb

THE TENTH MONTH, ORIGINALLY NAMED for the numeral eight on the first Roman calendar is sacred to the goddess Astera. As the daughter of Zeus and Themis, she lived on Earth during the Golden Age (correlating to the golden days of summer) and withdrew back to Mount Olympus at the end of the Golden Age. Thus, the chill of October correlates with Astera's withdrawal from Earth.

The Irish called the month *Deireadh Fomhair*, The Anglo-Saxons called it *Winterfelleth*, which means winter is coming. The Franks called it *Windurmanoth*, or Vintage Month, referring to the harvest of grapes for wine. And the backwoods people call it Hunter's Moon. The birthstones of October are opal and tourmaline. The flower of October is the calendula. There is often a warm time in October known as second summer or Indian Summer in the United States. It is also called Saint Bridget's Summer by the Swedish, Saint Theresa's Summer in Italy, Saint Gall's Summer in Germany and Switzerland, and the Summer of Saint Luke in England. This is the month of fertilizing fields in preparation for next summer's harvest, a colorful time of slow withdrawal into winter.

OCTOBER 1, **Heart.** *My heart is the center of my being, the center where my understanding meets the challenges that present themselves. It is where my inner child meets my adult and my higher awareness. I bring conflicting parts together in the garden of my heart and am at peace.*

Heart of Peace Meditation

1. Sit comfortably and close your eyes.

2. Imagine that there is a garden in your heart. This is your special place. No one else need come here unless you invite them. Notice whether you have a boundary around your heart or not. If you have nothing separating your heart from the outside world, imagine that you could build one if it feels right. It may be a circle of trees; it may be a hedge row or a stone wall, whatever you desire and feels right for you.

3. Invite in your higher self, your inner family, (mother, father, or child). Notice these relationships and notice their familiarity with one another. Now invite in your allies. Notice that some might be animals or spirits.

4. Invite in the two or more parts of yourself that are in conflict. Just be with them. Then listen to the dispute. Hear all each has to say.

5. When you are ready, ask for a solution to the conflict to be presented. Be with what is. It may come from a surprising source.

6. When the solution is agreed upon or everyone shifts into alignment, thank everyone for coming and let them go. Be with yourself and your inner family knowing you can come back any time your wish.

7. If you had no resolution, your image went blank or black, or you

could not maintain your concentration, you may need some support in completing this exercise. Ask someone you trust to assist you in going into your heart. You may need to find a counselor, therapist, hypnotist, or healer to help you. Also try surrounding yourself with gold light before you begin. Take the time you need in each step and do not rush the process.

OCTOBER 2, **Help.** *I practice receiving. I can ask for help when I need it.*

There is no shame in not knowing how to go about something. When you ask for help from others, you give them an opportunity to complete their purpose and offer their wisdom.

OCTOBER 3, **Colorful.** *I enjoy the colors of autumn. I allow the colors to stream forth into my heart and feed my soul. These colors of gold, red, yellow, and orange are full of vibrancy. I take in the vibrancy of color.*

OCTOBER 4, **Cool.** *As the weather changes, I notice the coolness of the season and the changes that come with the approaching winter weather. I notice the places in myself where I am feeling cool and warm toward myself and others.*

OCTOBER 5, **Changes.** *This is a time of many changes in the weather, as well as changes in myself. I notice what needs changing, and I give my attention to it. I am at peace sorting and letting go.*

OCTOBER 6, **Productive.** *Fall helps me focus on where I can be productive. The cooler weather gives me motivation to hunker down and complete tasks that help me be more productive.*

〰〰 Breathing Together 〰〰

What better meditation than breathing together with your lover in a spoon position? When you match your breath with your lover's, inhaling at the same time and exhaling just a little longer than he or she, there is a powerful physiological and emotional resonance. Besides being calming, it helps you both fall asleep easily.

OCTOBER 7, **Harsh.** *Sometimes the harshness of encroaching winter shows itself. Sometimes my harshness or the harshness of others is an obstacle to my growth. I notice today what is harsh and rough in myself.*

OCTOBER 8, **Radiant.** *In my heart lies my radiance. In every cell of my body, light is the foundation life force. Today I allow myself to feel radiant.*

Prayer for the Loved Ones

To be said while lighting candles:

We begin by honoring the Light.

We light these candles for our families, our beloveds, our friends, for all our relations;

For those who are near and for those from whom we feel an unwanted distance;

For the newborn, and the elderly, and for all the wounded children.

*May the candles inspire us to use our powers to heal and not harm,
to help and not hinder, to bless and not curse.*

*May their radiance pour out upon our hearts and spread light into the
darkened corners of our world.*

—adapted from a Passover Haggadah by Rachel Altman
and Mary Jane Ryan

OCTOBER 9, **Perplexity.** *Being with what perplexes me, I can allow the
answers to emerge. Sometimes I have to go in reverse, backing away from the
problem that perplexes me before I can go forward. I am resting with what
perplexes me.*

OCTOBER 10, **Humility.** *Today I listen to others for wisdom, and I am
transformed.*

Humility is not a word well known by western minds. Humility is really
listening to others, desiring their viewpoint. It is being ready for change,
supporting the idea that we do not have all the answers. It is the ability
to learn from others rather than demonstrating at every minute that we
are top dogs. It is allowing for the fact that we can be like a child listening for greater understanding.

Ceremony for Natural Disasters

In California, October seems to be the month of natural disasters. It has
been the time of big fires, such as the 1989 Loma Prieta earthquake, and
is often the last month before the floods begin. In honor of the changes
that citizens of California go through, here is ceremony for natural

disasters. Remember, different disasters require different actions and rites. The following questions might help you:

1. How can I reclaim balance with the elements?
2. What will help me feel safer?
3. What is my instinct telling me I need to do to heal?
4. Who do I want to join me?
5. Where is the most appropriate place to hold my ritual?

Once you feel ready, you might want to create a circle, enclosing the remaining possessions after the fire, flood, or other disaster. One by one you might give thanks for what remains, then ask for help regarding what to do next.

OCTOBER 11, **Perseverance.** *Today I continue to persevere as part of the process of my unfolding path. I allow myself to breathe ease into every step.*

Our ancestors knew about perseverance. They lived closer to the elements, closer to the will of nature. Perseverance means continuing with the intention of living in the midst of survival. They persevered to make a home, find a place or keep a place, and have a life for their families. Perseverance is never giving up on a goal, even in the midst of hardship. Think of a goal or a quality you have achieved, and congratulate yourself.

OCTOBER 12, **Rigor.** *Today I look at the rigor in my life, where it serves me, where it doesn't, and how I really want my days to unfold in a sacred manner.*

October is the month when the rigorous weather sets in. The leaves are changing color, and we get ready for winter. Sometimes the rigor of our schedules wreaks havoc on our energy level and our ability to enjoy our friends and family. It's important to make sure we aren't overextending ourselves.

OCTOBER 13, **Protection.** *Today I look at protection in my life, where I might give safety, and where I might choke off life from too much protection.*

Keeping something safe from harm is important, keeping something too safe for growth is something else. While protection is important, smothering actually chokes off the life force.

OCTOBER 14, **Friendship.** *Today I let my friends know I care.*

What can be better than a friend? Someone to know you and to love and care for you when everyone else seems to be too busy to listen. Friends show up. They pay attention and rarely judge. When they give their opinion, even if it is hard to hear, they mean it to serve you. The Greeks called it *agape,* or brotherly love

Friendship Ritual

Our friends are so important in the fabric of our lives. We gain support from friends that can get us through anything. But how often do we tell them that they are important to us? Here is a little ritual for that.

With a group of friends, hold a gathering. This doesn't have to be a large group. One or two friends works more intimately than a large crowd.

1. When you are finished catching up with one another's lives, ask the group to form a circle.

2. Set a chair of honor at one place in the circle. You can cover it with a beautiful fabric to make it fancy.

3. Begin by saying something like, "I have gathered you together to honor each of you in my life. You have seen me through a great deal, and I want to say thank you."

4. Then bring out a large bowl and a pitcher of warm water with a large towel and some soap. You may want to use perfumed oil or some other fragrance.

5. Wash the feet of each of your guests. Massage their feet in the oil or perfume of your choice.

6. While you are washing, let them know what you love about them.

7. When you are finished, complete the gathering by giving yourselves a group hug.

OCTOBER 15, **Economy.** *Today I look with a graceful eye on the economy of my life and give attention to what needs more support.*

While usually thought of as dealing with money, economy can also refer to the monitoring of life force. It can mean knowing when enough is enough, whether it is money, time, or eating too many cookies.

OCTOBER 16, **Illusion.** *Today I sharpen my discernment and cut through illusion with the sword of truth.*

There can be illusion on many levels: spiritual, mental, emotional, and physical. Cutting through illusion takes a discerning eye, a sharp mind, and an open heart.

OCTOBER 17, **Foresight.** *Today I exercise foresight by going within and asking what is right for me.*

While living sacredly is concerned with being in the moment, foresight keeps us moving along the path of awareness regarding where we choose to step next.

OCTOBER 18, **Wings**. *Today I look with love on my wings and stretch them to see a broader view.*

Our spirits have wings that can fly over challenging situation to help us see things from different vantage points. Have you ever thought how many different kinds of wings there are? From dragonflies, to eagles, to hummingbird wings, to bat wings, there are as many ways to fly as there are types of animals to soar.

OCTOBER 19, Justice. *Today I rest in the knowledge that, although I cannot see justice at every point of my life, I can feel that it is working as the wheel of life turns.*

Some say that the law of Karma, the law of "do unto others as you would have them do unto you," is a form of universal justice. How does your perspective on a hurt or slight change when you consider this?

OCTOBER 20, **Sincerity.** *Today I listen for the authentic in speech and action.*

Genuine feelings and thoughts go to the core of who we are and deeply touch something we know is true. When someone says something to us with sincerity, there is no mistaking their meaning. Resolve to speak with sincerity.

OCTOBER 21, **Secret.** *Today I listen for the jewel in my heart and the hearts of those I love.*

Inside each of us there is a place few people ever get a chance to know. It is usually kept hidden. This secret place holds an essence of our being, shared deeply only in silence, like a jewel glowing in our hearts that resonates with the jewel in another heart.

OCTOBER 22, **Flame.** *Tonight I light a candle just to ponder the flame, and then I rest in peace.*

For eons, whether around campfires or dinner tables, fire has brought people together sharing stories, laughing, or meeting over important decisions. A flame is such a reflective element of nature. When we look at a flame, we see passion—or hearts burning deeply within—or we see our thoughts. Something is knitted together in the dance of a flame.

OCTOBER 23, **Grace.** *Today I am aware of grace as a gift in my life.*

There is a quality of grace that is like a gentle gust of wind. It lifts your spirits, changes things around, and makes way for new things to appear in your life.

OCTOBER 24, **Health.** *Today I savor my health and enjoy my body, nourishing it, exercising it, stretching it, and loving it.*

Some say there is nothing better than to be in good health. Yet often when we have good health we take it for granted. Can you take a moment to be grateful for the good health you have been given?

OCTOBER **25**, **Balance**. *Today I stay in balance and watch for order in my life through harmony.*

OCTOBER **26**, **Heart**. *Today I look with my heart at the world around me. When I bring my thoughts into my heart they are transformed by love. My heart is the center of all the parts of my mind and body.*

～～ Retreat Day ～～

Take a retreat day for yourself. Pack a simple picnic lunch for one and go to a park, or take yourself out to lunch. Or if you prefer, stay at home and let the answering machine take your calls. Do not answer the phone for anything. You can also take yourself to the beach, if you have one near by. If you are a woman, try a retreat day the first day of your menstrual cycle. It really helps to clear the mind and focus your creativity. Do only things you love doing for the whole day. Read a book, draw a picture, listen to your favorite tunes, or go fishing!

OCTOBER **27**, **Solitude**. *Today I listen to my heart garden and rest in the peace I find there.*

A necessary element for anyone who is involved in creativity, solitude
is not very well understood or practiced by most people. In order to
have an inner life and an inner dialogue, however, we must allow ourselves to be in solitude from time to time. How long has it been since
you were alone?

OCTOBER 28, **Melancholy.** *Today I give myself permission to go within
and feel what I feel.*

Autumn can bring on feelings of melancholy. Many call it seasonal
depression. When we remember that this is the season of hibernation
for many animals, it seems appropriate to help ourselves go within.
Perhaps it is time to go in and let ourselves feel what we are feeling.

OCTOBER 29, **Boundaries.** *Today I look at areas in my life where I need to
set boundaries. I respect the boundaries of others.*

In setting boundaries, we make ourselves heard and clarify our needs.
They can be set with sharpness and severity or with gentleness.

OCTOBER 30, **Intimacy.** *Today I relish those times of intimate contact with
others, and I am grateful.*

There are many ways to experience intimacy. Sharing poems and stories
are forms of intimacy. Touching and being loved, spending time together
at the beach or in woods or simply sharing your day alone together can
all be forms of intimacy.

~~~ An Altar Honoring the Dead ~~~

This Halloween, try your own version of the Celtic altar. Lay out on a buffet or countertop a cloth, some candles, and photos of those loved ones who have passed on. Then light the candles at sunset and share stories with your family. If you are alone, talk to the photos as if your family members were still present, resolving grief, sharing hopes or wishes, or whatever you choose. Give yourself as much time as you need.

Pretend that you are connecting with the Earth through roots that grow out your feet. Let the roots grow deeply into the Earth connecting all the way into the center. Draw this energy up from the Earth, bringing it into your heart through your legs. Then send a cord up through your throat and out of your head, all the way to the sun. Now bring your attention back down the cord and into your heart. Mix all three energies together.

OCTOBER 31, **Grief.** *I am grateful for my tears. They support me in the process of living more fully.*

Grief is a gift to help let go of past hurts. It allows us to reconcile our feelings with our bodies and belief systems. The poet Rumi said of grief, "Your grief for what you have lost lifts a mirror up to where you are bravely working."

Halloween

Today is Halloween, or All Hallows Eve, the European version of the Mexican Day of the Dead. It is the night before All Saint's Day, the day of the year when the veil is the thinnest, and we have more direct communication with those who have gone before us.

In the Celtic tradition, people spread out an altar with photos of the dead on it, along with fruit (such as a pomegranates, apples, or grapes), and candles. Friends gather and they tell stories together about their relatives and remember them.

Of course, it's also a time for children to dress up in ghoulish costumes and roam the streets for tricks or treats. This seems like a healthy way for children to face the reality of death. It is also a festival of being contrary. A time to do what is opposite of what is socially acceptable. A night to honor the trickster. So go for it!

November

No one knows how, what changes, changes . . .
—Rumi, translated by C. Barks

NAMED FOR THE ROMAN NUMBER NINE, when it was the ninth month on the original Roman calendar, November is now the eleventh month. The Roman guardian of this month is Cailleach the veiled woman or the Old Woman Goddess. Red is the color of November in the Celtic tradition, honoring the woman trilogy (Mother, Maiden, and Crone), for the blood of life and the blood of women is honored by the color red.

The Egyptians called this the Month of Isis, whose husband Osiris was dismembered. She collected his body parts and brought them together again between November 1 though November 3. This story is connected with the dismembering of the warmth and the return to darkness.

Many other cultures see this month as a time of surrender and return to the dark days of winter. The Northwest Coast Indians, for example, have a teaching story called *Salmon Boy*, which is about a father symbolically slaying his salmon son to become an adult, after he has experienced his adolescence in the deep sea.

Called by the Anglo-Saxons *Blotmonath*, or Blood Month, this is a time of sacrifice in honor of all those livestock that could not make it through the winter. It was also called *Herbistmanoth* Harvest Month by the Franks. The Celts call it *Samhain* (sow-ain) or All Saint's or *La Shambna*, which is the first day of the Celtic calendar and the first day of the month. The month is referred to as Beaver Moon or Fog Moon in backwoods traditions.

The topaz is the stone of November, which honors true friendship, and chrysanthemum is the flower. November being the first fierce weather month, is a time acknowledging the underworld and the cycles of life and death.

NOVEMBER 1, **Independence.** *My soul is free to express itself to those I love. It is free to choose what is right for me, whether or not others agree. Today I feel the independence of my spirit in all things.*

All Saint's Day

This is the time to commemorate the dead. In ancient pagan festivals, this season of letting go begins traditionally with bonfires, known as tinley fires, which purify for the coming winter, light the way to the underworld, and dispel fear. The Christian celebration commemorates the lives of the saints.

To your altar of relatives who have passed, add today any candles or pictures of saints who you wish to commemorate. Saints have become symbolic through their work for particular causes. For example, Saint Francis lived in harmony with nature, Saint Theresa's life was an example of service, and Hildegaard of Bingen was a mystic, scientist, and musician.

Take the image of your favorite saint and try this meditation. Take three or four deep breaths, going into your heart center. Imagine that you are in a green field, and the saint of your choice is walking toward you. She has her arms out stretched to you. Receive a gentle hug from the saint. Carry on a conversation with her. Ask her whatever you like. Ask for help with a problem you are facing.

Let her give you advice. Thank her with a gift if you wish. Take a few deep breaths and come back from the meditation gently.

NOVEMBER 2, **Gathering.** *Today I gather myself together in celebration of my inner family.*

Whether we gather crops from the harvest or a group of friends for a celebration, this season speaks of gathering, sharing, and celebration.

All Souls Day

Today is a day for those souls in the Christian tradition not elevated to sainthood. Add to your altar those people in your life who were teachers. If you do not have their photos, write their names on a piece of paper.

Try this meditation. Sit or stand in front of your altar. Light your candles and list the things you learned from each person pictured in front of you. Say a prayer of thanks for the lessons and the teachers.

NOVEMBER 3, **Comfort.** *I am comforted at this time of year with good food, friends and the warmth of home. I remember today those who may not be so fortunate.*

A Womanhood Celebration

Because the spirit of November is about the feminine principle, here is a womanhood celebration that can help you honor femininity. It is a chance to let go of the past, embrace the future, and reflect on personal growth. To begin, ask yourself some basic questions:

What does it mean for you to be a woman?

What are the qualities you want to release from the past (for example: impatience, judgment, procrastination, and so on)?

What are the new qualities that you want to express or continue into womanhood (for example: desire, playfulness, creativity, inner beauty)?

Are the qualities you have chosen helping you become more of yourself?

Who would you like to help you celebrate your transition?

What objects would you like to use that have meaning for you? (This could be jewelry, hair ornaments, pieces of cloth, or something from your mother or grandmothers.)

What elements are necessary to include in this rite (earth, air, fire, and water)?

Where would you hold such an event?

How would you like to open the ritual?

What would you declare and embrace as the center of the ritual?

What would you choose to represent the qualities you are letting go of and taking hold of?

You might want to write them down on a slip of paper, burn the negative ones, and plant the positive ones in a houseplant so that every time you water the plant you are giving life to those qualities.

How would you close your ritual?

~~~ **Getting Out of Your Head Meditation** ~~~

Do you ever have trouble stopping your mind from racing on to the next task? Try this: Place your palm on the back of your neck and breathe into it. Let your energy drop out of your head and into your heart. Take at least ten deep breaths. Another way to stop your mind is to exchange head massage with someone. Start near the forehead, rubbing slowly in small circles. Don't forget to breathe deeply. Sighs are welcome!

NOVEMBER 4, **Surrender.** *This is the season of letting go. Today I surrender to the flow of life and allow my spirit to rest on the tide.*

NOVEMBER 5, **Wind.** *I am grateful for the wind. I release my cares into it.*

Like grace, the wind is sometimes a whisper of gentleness, hardly noticed when it begins, but profoundly felt like the touch of a healing hand. At other times it can be wild and harsh. Today, notice the winds of change in your life.

NOVEMBER 6, **Patience.** *Today I notice where I need more patience and let the spirit of autumn, of the unknown, help me let go.*

Everything requires patience to unfold, from a bud of a flowering plant to a child, to a new relationship or career. What do you need to do to have more patience?

NOVEMBER 7, **Dreams.** *Listening to the dreams of autumn, I am aware that this is a season of letting go and of mystery. I listen for the mystery of life to speak through my dreams. I am grateful for this, and I am open to what it is teaching me.*

NOVEMBER 8, **Silence.** *Deep at the heart of mystery is silence. It is a wellspring of wisdom, of being, of knowing. I rest in the silence.*

NOVEMBER 9, **Release.** *When I cry it is healing. I let myself feel what it is I need to release.*

Sometimes the silence brings up things in our lives that need to be released. Sometimes tears are the lubricant for release. Here's a ritual to help.

Ritual of Release

By yourself or with a group of friends, take a bunch of balloons and a large hat pin. Set your intention to release a quality or challenge at a time, then pop a balloon. Balloons could be used for a variety of other purposes, such as to release fears or sadness dealing with other losses, relationships, or moving. Although these sound like very different reasons to use balloons, there is loss in every transition, an ending in each new beginning.

NOVEMBER 10, **Curiosity.** *Today I let the season surprise me.*

Part of the unknown is the element of surprise. Colors can be surprising and so can storms and challenges. Why not see this season of the unknown through the eyes of a child who is curious and excited for the next surprise?

NOVEMBER 11, **Union.** *Today I look for places to build bridges bringing together a unique union.*

Joining two halves is one way to think about union. But it can also mean joining two wholes, as in countries or counties that are separate and join a union, or two people when they are joined in love. Bridging can be a significant way to bring about union. In this way, one tends not to lose autonomy, and it allows for the union from strength.

NOVEMBER 12, **Good Wishes.** *Today I give the simple gift of good wishes and spread some joy around.*

It is amazing how different the world looks when we can spread good wishes to others or receive them for ourselves.

For Women Older Than 50

Here's a ritual to try with friends. You can make this a Crone (wise woman) Ceremony for yourself or an older friend.

1. Form a circle and open with a prayer and blessing. You may want to state: "This is my crone ceremony. Today I am being initiated into my wisdom years." You may want to lay out the format to those in the group. Ask someone in the group ahead of time to create a special prayer for you. Then hold a giveaway, where gifts to those who come are of special meaning as in the Native American Northwest Coast tradition.

2. Invite everyone to share a story from their life experience as a mother, maiden, or crone. Have a hoop set up as a loom and a basket of yarn and cloth. Invite everyone to weave their favorite colors into the loom as they speak.

3. Ask the guests who are left to hold a space in prayer for you while you go through your initiation. In a room in your house, invite three women who you have chosen as elders to assist you. They will ask two questions, "What are you letting go of today?" and "What are you invoking for yourself?" Then they speak your name (it could be a sacred name for yourself). Allow them to bathe you in rose-scented water and dress you in new robes. Let them give you bits of wisdom from your tradition or from native African, Native American, and Earth-based traditions if that suits you. They can pass on secrets to you, share something they learned only in their later years, or give you a gift. When they are done, they can present you to the waiting guests, stating your name (a new one if you choose) as your friends form a long tunnel, which you walk through. To conclude the day, you may want to share a potluck feast together.

〜〜 Menstruation Meditation 〜〜

A woman's menstrual flow is a mystery. Every month we bleed and don't die! The natural flow readies us to receive a seed like the fertile soil of the Earth. Take time to feel your body changing during this time of the month. Your energy is actually reversing itself in order to cleanse. No wonder you are out of sorts. Take time to rest; notice your dreams and visions at this time. Women are more sensitive, intuition is sharper, and creativity is flowing during menses. Take time to feel yourself connecting with Mother Earth. Imagine that you are releasing your blood back to her. She receives it gladly to nourish and nurture the Earth. Remember we are hers, not the other way around.

NOVEMBER 13, **Surprise**. *Today I surprise someone with joy, and I surprise myself in the process.*

There is nothing more fun than surprises, especially when they are loving. Giving a gift for no particular reason, showing up in helpful ways, or letting someone know you care can make a delightful surprise.

NOVEMBER 14, **Foolishness**. *Today I give myself the opportunity to be foolish.*

When life gets too serious, it is healthy to be foolish, to let yourself be silly, to give yourself time to heal from big decisions and challenges.

NOVEMBER 15, **Song**. *Today I let my inner child sing his/her song again.*

Finding your voice in song can be a very important healing journey for many people. When did you stop singing?

NOVEMBER 16, **Play**. *Today I give myself permission to be playful. I take myself out to a place that I enjoy playing. What is stopping you from enjoying life? Write your answer on a slip of paper and burn it in the fireplace.*

NOVEMBER 17, **Judgment**. *Today I release my judgments of myself and others and support their unfolding process.*

Sometimes the hardest judgment we make is on ourselves. Judgments always separate and condemn. While discernment is necessary to evaluate what is true for us and what is not, judgment is not necessary.

NOVEMBER 18, **Process.** *Today I relish the process of my unfolding journey.*

We can set all sorts of goals, draw roadmaps, and chart our future. Goals once reached are quickly forgotten. What we do not forget, however, is the journey, one step at a time.

NOVEMBER 19, **Success.** *Today I congratulate myself for my successes and adjust my goals.*

There are many forms of success, some have to do with accomplishing goals. Other successes have to do with our values and meeting, with integrity, what we cherish. Sometimes we are successful when we have conveyed an important message to our children or gotten across what we need to communicate to a colleague or loved one. Perhaps we are successful with a diet that we have been trying to stay on, or an exercise plan.

Success Support

Sometimes, we struggle with feelings of success and failure. They are actually two sides of the same coin. Fear of success is often tied to fear of increased responsibility. Fear of failure is often tied in with feelings of shame or humiliation. Although it is easy for most of us to harass ourselves for our failures, it is not always easy to congratulate ourselves for our successes. Take a moment and list some accomplishments that help you feel good about yourself. It does not have to be job related. Let it flow out of you. Write as long as you need to. Take the next several days until Thanksgiving and write down your daily successes.

〜〜 Acknowledging Your Teachers 〜〜

Either in your journal or on a large sheet of cardboard, name the important teachers in your life, whether actually classroom teachers or friends, circumstances, even difficulties. Give some space to each one and draw, write, or paint about what each gave to you. Give voice to what you are honoring in them that has helped you. If it is appropriate, let the people who have been teachers for you know how much you appreciate them in a letter. If it is an illness, like cancer, or a stroke, write what you have learned from the experience. You may want to post these lessons somewhere in your home, on a mirror, in your closet, or on the wall over your altar, to honor the challenge.

NOVEMBER **20**, **Teaching**. *Today I listen for the next teaching. I am ready for the lessons.*

We are all teachers to each other. Sometimes we learn from our children, sometimes from our elders, and sometimes from our enemies or illnesses.

NOVEMBER **21**, **Enthusiasm**. *Today I live sacredly by being enthusiastic.*

When we bring enthusiasm to a project or to life, we are bringing life force or spirit to what we are doing. The original word dates back to the Greeks *en* meaning in and *theos* meaning God, also *ergo* meaning in God or God possessed.

NOVEMBER 22, **Bonding**. *I honor the people, animals, and places on the Earth that give me a sense of belonging.*

We all need to feel connected to life. Babies without a sense of bonding die. Isolation is part of our American cultural pathology. Who can you reach out to today?

NOVEMBER 23, **Completion**. *I allow myself to draw to completion those projects that I need to finish. I look at the areas where I am completing things and where I need to honor the loose ends.*

Sometimes endings are difficult for us to master. Although we want projects or challenges to come to a close, there is always that final letting go that is challenging.

NOVEMBER 24, **Affection**. *Today I share affection with those I love. I am grateful for those with whom I can be affectionate.*

It is a gift to give and a gift to receive. Sometimes a hug is all we need to turn our day around.

NOVEMBER 25, **Unknown**. *Today, I allow myself to be in awe of the unknown, letting myself feel its beauty and mystery.*

When we look at the stars in the sky, we never think much about the vast darkness that extends beyond them. We are so like the night sky.

We know our likes and dislikes. But so much of ourselves has yet to be discovered.

NOVEMBER 26, **Hospitality.** *I relax in the preparations and welcome in the spirit of the season, which is gratitude, togetherness, and thanksgiving.*

Preparing for feasts and gatherings—baking, cooking, and decorating—can be a wonderful delight to the senses. There is nothing more fun than to host a gathering of people in your home—and nothing more nerve-racking. If you can let go of some of the details and relax in generosity of the season, you can let go of the tension and feel the joy.

NOVEMBER 27, **Family.** *Today I give thanks for my family, whether it is my blood family or my spiritual family. I am grateful for the lessons and the gifts.*

Our family are our teachers. Each of us learns the most challenging and wonderful lessons from them. Some relative may be not-so-pleasant mirrors of our own nature. When we can forgive and accept our families for who they are and not try to make them into what we would like, we can be grateful. Here is a winter soup that your whole family will love.

Susan's Thai Coconut Soup
2 vegetable bouillon cubes or 4 cups fresh broth
2 tablespoons lemon grass, fresh or dried
½-inch chunk of fresh ginger, peeled and sliced
3 carrots sliced
1 large leek, white part only, sliced
½ small head white cabbage, sliced
1 1-inch chunk of fresh ginger peeled and sliced
⅓ pound brown mushrooms, sliced

1 15-ounce can lowfat coconut milk
Juice from ½ lemon
dash cayenne pepper to taste
salt to taste

Put the bouillon or broth, lemon grass, and ginger in a stew pot and bring to a boil. Cover and simmer for one to one and a half hours. Strain out ginger and lemon grass, then return broth to pan. Add remaining ingredients and simmer until just heated through. Serves 4–6.

〜〜 Thanksgiving 〜〜

The last Thursday in November in the United States is Thanksgiving, a time when people of every tradition celebrate and give thanks for the abundant harvest. Foods such as turkey, yams, potatoes, squash, cranberries, and pumpkin pies represent foods that were part of the original feast that the Indians and the Pilgrims shared after the first summer of harvest. Historically, it took more than six different groups of pilgrims from Europe over a period of several years to actually survive a winter on this continent. The Pilgrims found they had to make peace with the Indians, who then showed them superior methods of cultivation and home building, before a group was able to survive an entire winter.

NOVEMBER **28**, **Thanks.** *Today I remember the countless gifts I have been given, and I give thanks.*

When we remember to give thanks, we set in motion the cycle of grace, of receiving the answers to our prayers.

NOVEMBER **29**, **Charity.** *Nothing is given without the gift of receiving. Today I give and receive from my gifts.*

NOVEMBER **30**, **Riches.** *I have the riches of life within me.*

A Self-discovery Meditation

It takes courage to be yourself. To get started, try this meditation. Have ready three large pieces of paper, crayons or markers, and a candle. It may be more natural for you to draw, sing, drum, write, chant, hum, or laugh your way into more of yourself. However you access your creativity is wonderful and unique for you.

1. Light a candle and sit quietly in front of it. Close your eyes and take a few deep and slow breaths. Let yourself go. On the winds of your breathing, imagine a feather drifting from the top of your head through your body to the base of your spine. Imagine you are seeing an animal running free and wild in your belly. What is it?

2. Now imagine you have a bird circling overhead. What is it? Let the two animals live freely inside you. How do they interact?

3. Without disturbing your inner discovery, take three separate pieces of paper and draw each of the animals on separate pieces of paper and then their combined interaction on a third.

4. Next look into your heart and see a garden there. Let the animals come together inside your heart garden. Imagine a very wise and loving being there helping the two animals know each other better. When you are ready, take three more deep breaths and slowly come back into the room. You can return any time to these three locations inside you, just by follow these directions.

5. To further explore these animals, ask yourself: What are their movements? Dance out the movements of each animal, allowing yourself the freedom to move as they would move. Write about your experiences. Use the encyclopedia or library or the internet to understand more about your animals.

6. As you work with them over time, your animals may change, depending on where you live and your experiences in life. The bird generally represents your higher self or wisdom nature. The other animals represent your creative and sexual energy. Studying them both can give you clues about your own nature. It can increase self-awareness and self-acceptance.

December

Outside, the freezing desert night.
This other night inside grows warm, kindling.

—Rumi, translated by Colman Barks

DECEMBER IS NAMED FOR THE TENTH MONTH in the original Roman calendar and also the goddess Decima—the middle goddess of the three fates. It is called the Cold Moon or Hunting Moon by backwoods folks, Holy Month or *Heilagmanoth* by the Franks, *Aerra Geola*, or the month before Yule, by the Anglo-Saxons, and *Mi na Nollag* or Christmas Month by the Irish.

Besides winter solstice, the month is also the time of the birth of many sun gods and saviors, including the Egyptian god, Osiris; Ball from the Syrians; Jesus of Nazareth; Apollo and Adonis from the Greeks; and Frey in the Norse tradition. The Scottish celebrate the New Year's festival of Hogmanay in December, which celebrates Hogmagog, their solar god. The birthstones of December are turquoise and zircon, and the flowers are poinsettia, holly, and narcissus.

DECEMBER 1, **Withdraw.** *Sometimes it is necessary to withdraw in order to feel what is necessary for the next step. Releasing my fears, I allow myself to withdraw when I need to, knowing that I will come back out when it is time to begin again.*

～～ Light Shower ～～

In the shower in the morning or evening, imagine that you are standing in a shower of light. Allow the energy from your highest and wisest source, from the archangels, or from God, as it pours through you from the top of your head through your body, through your legs, and into the Earth. Imagine your chakras lighting up like a rainbow of color from the crown-white, through the spectrum (violet—third eye, sapphire blue—throat, emerald green—heart, yellow—solar plexus, orange—second chakra, to red at the base). You can pray, "From the highest source of wisdom and light, I pray that my energy field, chakra system, mental body, and emotional body be flush, filled, and cleansed with light. Clean away any energy that is not mine, sending it back to its source. Thank you, Great Spirit, blessed be."

DECEMBER 2, **Balance**. *I find balance within myself in the way that works best for me.*

Some people experience balance as running from one extreme to the other. Some people simply slow down and experience their center. Others feel balance by being present to all the aspects of themselves and feeling their wholeness as balance. Some find balance with others, and some by being alone. You know what works best for you in your own way.

DECEMBER **3**, **Meditation**. *Sitting alone and in silence for a few minutes each day, I meditate to restore and rejuvenate myself and to stay in a listening mode with my inner guidance.*

DECEMBER **4**, **Clearing**. *Clearing away the old and stepping into the new, I see the necessity of beginning again. In clearing with others in my relationships, I can start again. In clearing my desk of bills and papers, I make way for the new month. In clearing up difficulty with my car, it runs better.*

DECEMBER **5**, **Wholeness**. *I am already whole. Every part of me is contributing to my wholeness. Even the parts I cannot love yet. Even the aspects of my character that I do not claim. Even the parts that I want to understand better. All are a part of me. I am perfect in my imperfection.*

DECEMBER **6**, **Decay**. *Today, I sit with what may be in decay in my life, with what may be sprouting, and with what may be ready for harvest.*

Honoring the Cycles of Life

Life cycles include death and decay as well as seeding, sprouting, flowering, fruiting, and harvest. So many people resist the death and decay part of their lives. But "to everything there is a season and a purpose" Ecclesiastes 3:1. Without this part of the cycle, we would not be able to regenerate into the new life that is awaiting us. Take a moment today and reflect on what in your life is decaying, what is seeding, and what is sprouting. Give yourself time enough to let your feelings out.

DECEMBER **7**, **Support**. *I watch where I am willing to receive support and where I have to do things myself. Letting go of having to do everything myself, I am more at ease asking and receiving the gift of support.*

〰〰 Hanukkah 〰〰

This is the eight-day feast of lights for the Jewish people celebrated beginning on December 29 in 1997, December 14 in 1998, December 4 in 1999, and December 22 in 2000. Hanukkah (or Chanukah) honors the rededication of the temple in Jerusalem in 165 B.C., after the defeat of the Syrians. Candles are lit on each of the eight days of the festival, with much dancing, feasting, and celebrating on the eighth night.

DECEMBER 8, **Obstacles.** *I recognize my obstacles and in recognizing them, I look for how I may have created or contributed to them. Seeing them as serving me, I can wait for a time when they will dissolve or shift. My obstacles are there to support my growth.*

The Empty Nest: A Ceremony for Letting Go

To honor December as the month of letting go and changes, here is a ceremony for the empty nest, but it can be used for any family transition. This rite assumes: 1) You are on speaking terms with your family; 2) You and your family members are willing to make changes together in your family dynamics. If you are not in a place with your family where you can work things out, maybe it is best to work by yourself or with those members of the family who are willing to share an experience like this with you.

If such a ritual is applicable, the first thing necessary is to be sure everyone in the family is willing to participate. If not, you may want to explore together what fears or resistance each member has around such a transition. You may decide among yourselves that some of you need a ritual and some of you don't. You may decide to proceed with those members who really want to be involved.

If you agree to go ahead, you may ask yourselves to individually write down the answers to the following questions:

1. What does this family mean to me? What are the aspects or qualities that I love and want to keep?

2. What do I need to release to accommodate this transition?

3. What other aspects would I like to see changed?

4. Are there aspects of my relationship that I want to continue with each member of my family?

5. If you don't want to continue a relationship in the family, ask yourself what hurts, angers, or resentments you carry. Perhaps you may need some help letting them go. If you don't want to release them, ask yourself, "What am I getting out of holding on to them?"

When you have made your lists, share them with each other if you wish. Then ask yourself:

1. If I were to give each person a symbolic gift representing the essence of that person or their role in the family, what would it be?

Together you may want to decide:

2. Of the immediate family, who will be present? Beyond the immediate family, who should be present?

3. Where do we want to hold the ritual?

4. How do we want to begin the ritual, what should be in the middle, and how do we want it to close?

5. Draw up a rough outline together, by deciding what is necessary to include. Don't get too locked into an outline or lists. If you speak from the heart, there will be room for spontaneity, humor, and fun as well as for warm feelings.

6. Set a date and time. Depending on where you hold the ritual, you may want certain elements. For example, if you choose to hold your ritual inside, you may want to focus the energy of the group by creating an altar in the center of the room. Lay a cloth on the floor or use a low table as a base. Ask each family member to bring an object that has meaning to them. You could also include a bowl of Earth, a candle, and a glass of water, representing the four elements, Earth, air, fire, and water. You may choose to include religious aspects such as symbols, favorite prayers, readings, and so on.

7. One by one take turns saying or reading what family means to you, then present one another with the objects that represent the change you are going through. Kathy, for example gave her adult son Kevin a feather to symbolize his need for movement outside the family circle. She gave her husband a rock to symbolize how he had been the foundation and stabilizing presence in the family.

In order for each family member to feel included in the changes that are taking place within the family, it is important that they contribute in some way. But, remember to keep it simple, especially if there are several people involved. You don't need a lot of segments to the ritual to make it a significant event for all of you. Just come from the heart.

~~~ Lighting Up December ~~~

Candles are a traditional symbol of hope and are used in many religious holidays at this time of the year. Here is a ceremony you can do as you sit down to dinner. In a candelabra or with various holders, light a candle a day for the first eight days of the month, or to coincide with Hanukkah or Advent. For each candle, as you light it, name a quality or attitude you would like to bring into the season such as, faith, hope, joy, grace, harmony, peace, love, or caring. You can come up with your own names, or you can use the names of family members or friends for each candle. A prayer during this time can be: "I light this candle, and in so doing, I light the quality of _____ (joy, peace, and so on) in our lives and in the world. Peace be with us."

DECEMBER **9**, **Mirror.** *Today I play with the idea of others being a reflection of me.*

Who is a mirror for you today? Who reveals something of yourself that you may not want to admit? Who is holding the teaching you have been waiting for?

DECEMBER 10, **Contemplate.** *Spending time alone to contemplate, I discover my need for deep rest and rejuvenation. I am grateful for the opportunity to meditate, to listen, to contemplate.*

DECEMBER 11, **Shifting.** *Like the Earth, I shift inside with new growth. I can feel the old breaking away and the new energies coming forth. I am grateful for this, and I wait to watch more of me emerging. I am grateful for the shifting.*

DECEMBER 12, **Presence.** *Today I pay attention to my presence and what I offer or do not offer to others. I recognize who I feel energized around, who is a positive source of encouragement, and who is sapping my strength.*

Grandmother Goddess Day

Honoring the grandmothers, great women, and goddesses from every tradition, including Mary, Diana, Isis, Ashtar, Hecate, Judith, Demeter, Kali, and Innana, is a way to honor the feminine principle that is one of three major aspects of universal energy. Whether we are male or female, recognizing the goddess within gives recognition to both feminine and masculine aspects of ourselves, the heart is the great integrator.

Look into your heart and invite your masculine and feminine aspects to be present. Invite your higher wisdom self into your heart and then the aspect of the god/goddess that you are most comfortable with. Notice his/her strengths. He/she has a gift for you. What is he/she offering you? Close by taking a few deep breaths and returning to the room.

DECEMBER 13, **Oracle.** *I look to my own nature to see what I need to know for today, to bring me greater understanding of myself.*

～～ Paying Attention Meditation ～～

Nature is a constant reflection of wisdom. The flight of birds or the appearance of a squirrel or skunk can bring us messages if we are paying attention. Who is an oracle for you today? Who can tell you pieces of information that you need to know? Who brings you this information? Are you listening? Perhaps it is a bird, an animal, a change in the shrubs near your home, or the flight of a flock of birds. Remember to pay attention to signs today. Ask for messages about a particular challenge or question for which you need an answer. Write down your intention in your journal. Before you go to bed, write down the things you noticed.

DECEMBER **14, The Unknown.** *Today I look at how comfortable I can be with what is not known and allow myself to rest with faith in the right outcome. This is the season of entering the unknown. It is the season of hope and faith.*

DECEMBER **15, Illuminate.** *With my increasing awareness, I illuminate the next steps for me. I can see more clearly and look beyond appearances to what is more deeply revealed. My understanding illuminates with the light of my awareness.*

DECEMBER **16, Trickster.** *Today I recognize the trickster in me and in others, and I honor it for its lessons.*

Honoring the Trickster

The trickster is the part of ourselves that often does things in opposition to everything else. Signified by the court jester in Europe, the trickster in many indigenous tribal groups, the fool, or the god Loki in Norwegian mythology, helps us to understand that life is not always about the good, beautiful, and pure, as the pious would like us to believe. And it is not meant to be. The most challenging lessons often come to us in opposition to what is taught or popular or socially acceptable. In many cultures, the trickster is the most powerful teacher there is, often equated with the power of lightening. Take a moment to reflect on the trickster in your life. Who are the people, places, or events that brought sudden change or an opposite view? What in you is a trickster?

DECEMBER 17, **Revealed.** *I take my awareness from daily life, sit in silence, and listen to what is being revealed.*

Five Minutes of Listening

What is being revealed to you during this season of going into the dark part of the year? Always in the dark there is something we have not yet heard or seen. Always there is something to listen for, to release and collect. Take five minutes, sit in a comfortable chair, turn off the phone, and listen to the sound of your breath, to your heart beating. Create your inner sanctuary. It can be in grove of trees, by a lake, river, or the ocean, or in your own backyard. What do you hear welling up from within?

DECEMBER 18, **Surrender.** *I take a look at where I need to surrender in my life. I am grateful.*

Knowing that we do not hold all the answers, surrender is being open to other possibilities. It is giving ourselves to what is necessary and what is good for us, even though it always means letting go of preconceived ideas and plans.

DECEMBER 19, **Awe.** *The more I feel myself connected to the rhythms of life, the more I feel a greater sense of awe of all there is living around me and through me. I feel, see, and hold my awareness in this web of life today and experience my connection to the Great Spirit.*

～～ Mother's Night ～～

In the days of the Vikings, December 20 was called Mother's Night. This is a night to watch your dreams. On this night, dreams were to have foretold events of the coming year. Pay particular attention to your dreams this evening.

DECEMBER 20, **Sacred.** *I know that living the sacred every day is living as though my life were precious, and that I am precious to God as well, and that everyone I see and everything around me is precious also.*

Sacred living is about being with all that is in our lives, the ups and downs, the anger and joy—knowing that everything is a teacher.

Everything has something to offer. Living sacredly is slowing down enough to feel God and live according to our hearts. It is being aligned with the constant presence that is all around us supporting us in our life and affairs. It is knowing that nothing in our lives is outside of God—that life is a gift to be cherished.

Acknowledgments

I WOULD LIKE TO THANK Mary Jane Ryan, for her persistence and excellence, and most of all for her large heart, without which this book would not be in your hands. For the other wonderful folks at Conari Press, thank you. Special support came from "Kin Oyate" who inspired and deeply touched me with ceremony and monthly gatherings during my year and a half in my home town. Their dedication to living sacredly largely inspired this book. Great thanks to Roselyne Spolin and Seegar Gehrau, A. A. Michael, Susan Wolf, and Ernesto Lopez-Molina for your patience, love, and guidance while writing *Sacred Living*.

Bibliography

Arguelles, Jose. *The Mayan Factor: Path Beyond Technology.* Santa Fe: Bear and Co., 1987.

Arrien, Angeles, Ph.D. *Signs of Life: The Five Universal Shapes and How to Use Them.* Sonoma, CA: Arcus Publishing, 1992.

_____. *The Four-Fold Way: Walking the Path of the Warrior, Teacher, Healer and Visionary.* San Francisco: HarperSanFrancisco, 1992.

Bach, Edward, M.D. *The Bach Flower Remedies.* New Caanan: Keats Publishing, Inc., 1979.

Beattie, Melody. *The Language of Letting Go.* New York: Hazelden, 1990.

Beck, Renee and Sydney Barbara Metrick. *The Art of Ritual.* Berkeley: Celestial Arts, 1990.

Brown, Dee Alexander. *Bury My Heart at Wounded Knee.* New York: Holt, Reinhart, & Winston, 1970.

Budapest, Zsuzsanna. *The Goddess in the Bedroom.* San Francisco: HarperSanFrancisco, 1995.

_____. *The Holy Book of Women's Mysteries.* Berkeley: Wingbow Press, 1989.

_____. *Grandmother Moon: Lunar Magic in Our Lives - Spells, Rituals, Goddesses, Legends, & Emotions under the Moon.* San Francisco: HarperSanFrancisco, 1991.

_____. *The Grandmother of Time: A Woman's Book of Celebrations, Spells, and Sacred Objects for Every Month of the Year.* San Francisco: HarperSanFrancisco, 1989.

Campbell, Joseph. *Hero with a Thousand Faces.* Princeton: Princeton University Press, 1949.

Creation Magazine. "Sex and the Spirit." Volume Three, Number Two, May/June 1987.

Easwaran, Eknath. *The Upanishads.* Tomales, CA: Nilgiri Press, 1995.

Eliade, Mircea, ed. *The Encyclopedia of Religion.* New York: Macmillan, 1987.

Essene, Virginia. *Secret Truths for Teens and Twenties.* Santa Clara, CA: S.E.E. Publishing, 1986.

Fox, Matthew. *Breakthrough: Meister Eckhart's Creation Spirituality in New Translation.* Santa Fe: Bear and Co., 1980.

_____. *Original Blessing.* Santa Fe: Bear and Co., 1983.

Ghost Horse, Buck. *Red Nation's Sacred Way.* Oakland: private publication, 1986.

Gibbs, Jeanne. *Tribes.* Santa Rosa: Center Source Publications, 1987.

Grualnik, David B. *Webster's New World Dictionary.* New York: Warner Books, 1983.

Harvey, Andrew and Anne Baring. *The Mystic Vision.* United Kingdom: Godsfield Press, 1995.

Hay, Louise L. *Meditations to Heal Your Life.* Carson: Hay House, 1994.

Higgler, Sister M. Inez. *Chippewa Child Life and Its Cultural Background.* Washington, D.C.: United States Printing Office, 1951.

Hirshfield, Jane, with Mariko Aratani. *The Ink Dark Moon: Love Poems by Ono no*

Komachi and Izumi Shikibu, and Women of the Ancient Court of Japan. New York: Vintage Books, 1990.

The Holy Bible. London, England: Burns & Oates, 1954.

Houston, Jean. *The Possible Human.* Los Angeles: J.P. Tarcher, 1982.

Jung, Carl G. *The Archetypes and the Collective Unconscious.* Princeton: Bollingen Foundation, 1969.

_____. *The Symbolic Life: Miscellaneous Writings,* vol. 18. Princeton: Princeton University Press, 1950.

Keller, Erich. *The Complete Guide to Aromatherapy.* Tiburon, CA: H.J. Kramer, 1991.

King, Serge. *Kahuna Healing.* Wheaton: Theosophical Publishing House, 1983.

Madhi, Louise, Steven Foster Caraus, and Merideth Little. *Betwixt and Between: Patterns of Masculine Initiation.* La Salle, Il: Open Court Publications,1987.

Miller, Alice. *Drama of the Gifted Child: The Search for the True Self.* New York: Basic Books, Inc., 1981.

Mitchell, Steven (translator). *The Enlightened Heart: An Anthology of Sacred Poetry.* New York: Harper and Row, 1989.

_____. *The Selected Works of Rainer Marie Rilke.* New York: Random House, 1982.

_____. *Tao Te Ching.* New York: Harper Perennial, 1995.

Moore, Thomas. *Rituals for the Imagination.* Dallas: The Pegasus Foundation, 1983.

Nelson, Gertrude Mueller. *To Dance with God: Family Rituals and Community Celebrations.* New York: Paulist Press, 1986.

Osho. *The Everyday Mediator: A Practical Guide.* Tokyo: Charles E. Tuttle, Inc., 1983.

Paladin, Lynda S. *Ceremonies for Change.* Walpole, NH: Stillpoint Publishing International, 1991.

Pearson, Carol. *The Hero Within: Six Archetypes We Live By.* New York: Harper and Row, 1986.

Pennick, Nigel. *The Pagan Book of Days: A Guide to Festivals, Traditions, and Sacred Days of the Year.* Rochester, VT: Destiny Books, 1992.

Perera, Brinton Sylvia. *Descent to the Goddess: A Way of Initiation for Women.* Toronto: Inner City Books, 1981.

Swami Prabhavananda. *The Song of God: Bhagavad-Gita.* Hollywood: Vendanta Society, 1969.

Reese, Lyn, et al. *I'm On My Way Running: Women Speak of Coming of Age.* New York: Harper and Row, 1980.

Rufus, Anneli. *The World Holiday Book: Celebrations for Every Day of the Year.* San Francisco: HarperSanFrancisco, 1994.

Starhawk. *The Spiral Dance.* New York: Harper and Row, 1979.

Swimme, Brian. *The Universe is a Green Dragon: A Cosmic Creation Story.* Santa Fe: Bear and Co., 1984.

Taylor, George M., *Talking with Our Brothers: Creating and Sustaining a Dynamic Men's Group.* Fairfax, CA: Men's Community Publishing Project, 1995.

Taylor, Robert, Susannah Seton, and David Greer. *Simple Pleasures: Soothing Suggestions & Small Comforts for Living Well Year Round.* Berkeley: Conari Press, 1996.

Thoele, Sue Patton. *The Woman's Book of Spirit*. Berkeley: Conari Press, 1997.

Underhill, Ruth M. *Red Man's America*. Chicago: University of Chicago Press, 1953.

Ven Gennep, Arnold. *The Rites of Passage*. Chicago: Phoenix Books, 1960.

Walker, Barbara G. *Women's Rituals: A Sourcebook*. San Francisco: Harper and Row Publishers, 1990.

Wall, Steve and Harvey Arden. *Wisdomkeepers: Meetings with Native American Spiritual Elders*. Hillsboro, OR: Beyond Words Publishing Inc., 1990.

Woodman, Marion. *The Pregnant Virgin: The Process of Psychological Transformation*. Toronto: Inner City Books, 1985.

Index

Born in Rockford, Illinois, and living today in Boulder Creek, California, Robin has been actively involved as an artist and writer for over twenty years. Her art work has been exhibited from California to New York. *Sacred Living* is her second book.

Beside writing prose, poetry, and painting for pleasure, Robin has studied and practiced energy healing throughout her adult life. Today she has a private practice as an intuitive counselor and energy healer. In private sessions, groups and workshops she uses her intuition to support people in their self-healing. Her intention is always to empower others in their personal growth and spiritual unfolding.

Robin is an experienced and sought-after speaker, workshop, and seminar leader. For information on her programs in sacred living, rituals, and personal growth, or to schedule a private session, please call (408) 338-1031.

Conari Press, established in 1987, publishes books on topics
ranging from spirituality and women's history to sexuality and
personal growth. Our main goal is to publish quality books
that will make a difference in people's lives—both
how we feel about ourselves and how
we relate to one another.

Our readers are our most important resource, and we
value your input, suggestions, and ideas. We'd love to hear
from you— after all, we are publishing
books for you!

For a complete catalog or to be added to our mailing list,
please contact us at:

CONARI PRESS
2550 Ninth Street, Suite 101
Berkeley, California 94710

800-685-9595   Fax 510-649-7190
e-mail conaripub@aol.com